I REMEMBER
LINDBERGH

John Grierson died the night of May 21, 1977, after giving
a lecture at the Smithsonian Institution in Washington,
D.C., in a commemorative symposium for the fiftieth anniversary of Charles A. Lindbergh's first solo transatlantic
flight to Paris. The lecture was a recounting of the ordeals of
the flight itself, much as they are told in this book. He had
arrived at the point in the story where Lindbergh had
reached Ireland. He was unable to continue his speech, sat
down quietly, and died a few hours later of a cerebral
hemorrhage. His death is a great loss to his family and
friends and to those who knew of him as one of the early
pilots of a heroic period in aviation. His last act was to pay
tribute to a fellow airman and to the profession in which he
himself had devoted his life.

Anne Morrow Lindbergh

June, 1977

I REMEMBER LINDBERGH

JOHN GRIERSON
Illustrated with photographs •
With an Introduction by ANNE
MORROW LINDBERGH

HARCOURT BRACE JOVANOVICH

NEW YORK AND LONDON

Library of Congress Cataloging in Publication Data
Grierson, John, 1909-1977.
   I remember Lindbergh.

   Includes index.
   SUMMARY: Flier John Grierson's personal recollections
of his friend Charles A. Lindbergh.
    1.   Lindbergh, Charles Augustus, 1902-1974—Juvenile
literature. [1.   Lindbergh, Charles Augustus, 1902-1974.
2.   Air pilots]   I.   Title.
TL540.L5G68   629.13′092′4   [B]   [92]   77-76436
ISBN 0-15-238895-8

First edition HBJ
B C D E F G H I J K

The author wishes to thank the following for permission to reprint
material in this book:
Charles Scribner's Sons for quotations from *The Spirit of St. Louis* by Charles
A. Lindbergh, copyright 1953 by Charles Scribner's Sons; John Murray Ltd.,
also for quotations from *The Spirit of St. Louis*; Cassell & Collier Macmillan
Publishers Ltd. for a quotation from *The Central Blue* by Sir John Slessor; the
Charles A. Lindbergh Family Papers, Yale University Library, for numerous
photographs.

Contents

Introduction

In the summer of 1933 my husband and I were making a survey flight around the North Atlantic in preparation for Pan American's first air service between America and Europe. In our Lockheed Sirius, equipped with pontoons, we had flown from New York to Labrador, Newfoundland, and Greenland, covering all possible landing sites for the air routes of the future. Having crossed the ice cap for the second time, on this occasion to Angmagssalik on the west coast, on August 15 we left Greenland on our way to Europe and landed in Iceland near Reykjavik. A young Britisher in a motorboat came out to greet us and very efficiently helped to steer our plane to a mooring. He seemed to know what he was about, both as to seaplanes and harbor conditions. He introduced himself as John Grierson and explained that he had flown to Iceland in a de Havilland Gypsy Moth seaplane on the first leg of a flight to America, following the Arctic route from east to west. He was too modest to tell us of his distinguished background of long-distance flying, and he looked far too young and boyish to have any such record.

(Looking back, I realize we were rather young ourselves.)

We stayed at the same hotel in Reykjavik, and I can remember how companionable it was to share flying experiences with this confrère. Long-distance aviators, in those days, were rare enough to form a kind of international brotherhood. We were, however, rather worried about the next leg of his proposed flight. The Gypsy Moth looked fragile next to our Sirius, and my husband wondered if Grierson knew what gale winds he might encounter in Greenland and the additional hazards he faced trying to cross the 10,000-foot ice cap in a machine of only 85 h.p.

Even in Reykjavik gale winds were a problem, and when Grierson finally tried to take off, his plane was overturned in the rough seas just outside the harbor. Since Pan American had a well-equipped base ship stationed in Reykjavik to back up our flight, the skilled mechanic on board was able to help him salvage the plane. Relieved that he was not hurt and that the dangerous flight was at least postponed, I recorded the incident in my diary: "I can't help feeling it's lucky. He is such a nice man."

Our concerns about our new friend were unjustified. John Grierson was no amateur pilot but a daring, experienced, and skillful long-distance flyer. He had graduated from The Royal Airforce College at Cranwell in 1929 and flown solo to India in 1930 in his own aircraft, a third-hand Gypsy Moth, named *Rouge et Noir*. In the same plane he established a record in 1931 by a flight from India to England, and in 1932 flew 9,000 miles across the U.S.S.R. to Samarkand. In fact, when we first saw *Rouge et Noir* in Iceland, it had flown over thirty-four different countries. In the year following the mishap we had witnessed in Reykjavik, Grierson, with true Scottish determination, acquired a larger aircraft, the Fox Moth seaplane, and tried this same flight again. The new plane, appropriately named *Robert Bruce*, on a third attempt, successfully made the first London-Ottawa flight and at the same time the first solo flight across the Greenland Ice Cap.

In our era of unlimited air travel these flights are daily routine, and it is almost impossible to put oneself back fifty years to this early period of flying and imagine its unexpected hazards, its continuous drudgery, its heart-breaking failures and its incredible triumphs. The late 20's and the early 30's spanned a short heroic period in aviation history after the early experimental trials of the pioneers and inventors, and before the practical implementation of commercial air routes. The men who took part in these long-distance flights and record-breaking hops were a special breed. They were not inventors or scientists, and they were not the gallant knights of World War I—or daredevils of the flying circus. They were men of courage and vision, the explorers of a new element, the passionate devotees of a craft they loved and the world it revealed to them, and, above all, they were ruggedly independent. They flew, for the most part, alone. They faced the myriad dangers clear-sightedly and could manage most emergencies single-handed. Because of the many unknowns of machines, weather, and territory, they relied more on their instincts than on their instruments.

Flying in those years was an art, not a science or a profession. The art was often handed down from one skilled artist to another almost in an apprenticeship, or it was learned by hard experience. The experts—like my husband and John Grierson—took chances, but their aims were practical, to prove the feasibility of world-wide air transportation. They did not court danger or death; they were incurably in love with life.

There are not many of this generation now left. The hazards of their occupation took a fair number. World War II claimed some of the best. And the normal process of aging and dying has thinned the remainder. John Grierson is one who survived the hazards and progressed through the swiftly paced stages of aviation's progress. He went early into civil aviation, holding a position as Operations Officer in the Air Ministry. During World War II he was a test pilot for Britain's first jet aircraft. In England's bleak years that followed the war he was a flight commodore for a whaling factory ship. Later he became a director of civil aviation for the British Zone of postwar Germany. And, true to his early commitment, he is still flying with the same zest as the young man in Reykjavik Harbor.

Fortunately, John Grierson has not only survived his many adventures but he has written about them in seven books. He knows whereof he writes. He experienced it all: the skittish machines, the battles with storms, fog, and ice, the uncharted terrain, the forced landings, the accidents, the delays, and the heady exhilaration of success. My husband and he had much in common, and when Grierson was writing a history of polar flight, the older airman agreed to write a foreword to his *Challenge to the Poles*. A later request when Grierson was participating in a historical aviation film received the forthright reply from my husband: "I do not know anyone I would rather cover my part than yourself." So it is with assurance I can affirm that I do not know of anyone better fitted to write *I Remember Lindbergh* than John Grierson.

John Grierson knew the era; he knew the machines; he knew the conditions and territories covered, and he knew the man. In my husband's words, "Only a man who flies can form words to fit an airplane's wings, and only one who has erred himself can touch with grace his brothers' errors." In fact, it is this latter critical faculty that brings a fresh and three-dimensional aspect to the well-known stories of my husband's flights in this brief period. Rereading John Grierson's evocation of that era I realize again how fortunate we were to be part of it and rejoice that younger readers can glimpse the early morning horizons of those hardy explorers and sense the warmth of companionship we shared—"We few, we happy few, We band of brothers."

Anne Morrow Lindbergh

April, 1977

Author's Note

On August 27, 1974, the day after Charles Lindbergh died, I wrote to John N. Irwin, then the United States ambassador to France, to suggest that he might interest the Fédération Aeronautique Internationale and the Aero Club de France in organizing an international memorial service for Lindbergh in Paris. A letter of acknowledgment, dated September 5, explaining that the ambassador was absent for a week, was soon followed by another letter saying that, because Ambassador Irwin's stay in Paris would soon be completed, he would not be able to participate in a memorial service, but the embassy wished me every success in my efforts. I then discussed the matter with Sir Peter Masefield, who suggested that a better idea would be to hold a Lindbergh memorial lecture at the Royal Aeronautical Society in London. Sir Peter submitted this idea to the president and council of the society, and they gave it their wholehearted support. In October they did me the honor of asking me to give a memorial lecture on May 21, 1975, the first anniversary after Lindbergh's death of his flight from New York to Paris in 1927.

Although I had been lucky enough to know Charles Lindbergh fairly well during his life—I met him and his wife, Anne, in Iceland in 1933—I had to do quite a bit of research in order to verify all the data necessary for such a historic lecture. I was able to obtain a lot of Lindbergh literature at the library of the Royal Aeronautical Society, and I traveled to the United States in order to review my project in detail with Anne Morrow Lindbergh. Anne took tremendous pains to help me at a time when she was deeply involved in the publication of a volume of her diaries and in the appalling amount of paperwork resulting from her husband's death. I also met with Juan Trippe, the former president of Pan American Airways, who had been closely associated with Lindbergh since 1929; Raymond Fredette, who was an intimate friend of Lindbergh and is now involved in writing his biography from the military point of view; and, at the National Air and Space Museum of the Smithsonian Institution, Donald Lopez kindly arranged a private viewing of the *Spirit of St. Louis* so that I could climb up and reach right into the cockpit.

Besides writing a sixty-minute lecture, I had to supply appropriate slides and documentary film in order to show my audience the hectic takeoff of the *Spirit of St. Louis* from Roosevelt Field, and the fantastic receptions Lindbergh had in Europe and when he returned to the states. The only disappointment in connection with the lecture was to come when, because the proofs for the Royal Aeronautical Society's journal, *Aerospace*, were not shown to me, there were various errors in the wording and the omission of any mention of the guest of honor. I am glad now to have the opportunity to put that right.

In addition to the absorbing and productive visit to America, my research included the pleasant necessity of flying to

Paris in my own airplane in order to meet Charles Lindbergh's elder daughter, Anne Lindbergh Feydy, who had kindly agreed to attend my lecture as representative of the Lindbergh family and guest of honor, for her mother unfortunately felt unable to come.

Owing to the snowy conditions we suffered in northern Europe in March, 1974, I had to postpone my first attempt to fly to Paris and heard that this had caused some disappointment to eight-year-old Charles Feydy, who was going to accompany his mother to Toussous-le-Noble, where he was most interested in seeing a collection of "fun" airplanes. When I eventually succeeded in dodging the snowstorms across Normandy, I was determined to make amends to young Charles by offering him a short flight.

Charles sat beside me, and as soon as we were properly airborne, I let him hold the controls. This was a novel experience for Charles because he was one of the few Lindbergh grandchildren who had never flown with Grandfather Charles. We proceeded westward to the south of Versailles, and all seemed to be going well until I looked back and realized that a snow flurry had obscured the airport with all the suddenness of an Antarctic storm. My radio direction indicators were not working very well, and because visibility was so poor, I called Toussous to ask for bearings, although I knew we were not far away. Thanks to the help of air traffic control, we groped our way back in heavy snow past Guyancourt into the Toussous circuit, and I was very relieved to land Charles and his mother, who, fortunately, appeared to be a good deal less alarmed by this experience than I was!

Young people must feel rather puzzled when they look back to the time in which a nonstop flight between New York and Paris was a world sensation, for today jumbo-jet loads of passengers are carried along that same route every day and night of the year. What do young people know of the solo triumph of Charles Lindbergh, and what do they know of the many other constructive things he did for aviation throughout his life? Of the many attributes Charles possessed, the key to all of them was the courage to meet a challenge. The challenge I am going to describe must be met by all persons of a new generation who, like young Charles, put their hands on the controls for the first time and look ahead into the unknown.

Chapter 1 ⬦ THE BOY

Charles Lindbergh's grandfather August was a lawyer and member of the Swedish Parliament. August emigrated to Minnesota in 1859 at the age of fifty, when Charles's father (also named Charles) was an infant. That was the age of ox-carts and prairie schooners, when travel was slow but often imperiled by accidents and ambushes, among other dangers. Indian raids were not uncommon—one of August's daughters was born in a stockade. August built a log cabin on the Sauk River, and the family faced an existence of hard work with little money to spare. Two years after the Lindberghs' arrival, August was injured in a freakish sawmill accident when he fell into the whirling blade, receiving a gash on his left arm and back. He was laid on a cushion in a hay wagon and taken over rough roads to his home, but no medical help was at hand. For three days, August seemed likely to die from infection and loss of blood. The doctor finally arrived on his horse, examined August, and had to amputate his arm and stitch up the wounded back. Still in great pain, August sat up and demanded to see his left arm before it was buried in a little coffin. "Taking the fingers in those of his right hand," wrote his grandson Charles in his best-selling book *The Spirit of St. Louis,* "he said slowly, in broken English, 'You have been a good friend to me for fifty years. But you can't be with me any more. So good-by. Good-by, my friend.' "

The accident had almost killed August Lindbergh, and it was of course months before he could work. The struggle to exist was now more difficult than ever. Just as soon as he could carry a gun, Charles's father was sent out to hunt. Fortunately, the hard life of those pioneers taught him the initiative and self-reliance that were to be invaluable Lindbergh family traits.

Charles's father received a law degree at the University of Michigan in 1883 and married a French-Canadian girl four years later. She died in 1898, leaving her husband with two little girls. In 1901 he married a teacher of Anglo-Scots-Irish ancestry. Evangeline Lodge Land Lindbergh was from Detroit, where, on February 4, 1902, she gave birth to Charles Augustus Lindbergh, Jr., who was to be her only child. The marriage of Charles and Evangeline was not very successful, perhaps because, as son Charles later wrote, "they were attuned mentally but not emotionally." They did not quarrel openly, however, and when Charles, Sr. became a congressman—when Charles, Jr. was five—his wife did everything possible to keep up appearances by, for example, regularly taking their son to church, which was considered politically advantageous to a congressman. Sometimes they followed Congressman Lindbergh to Washington, but in the summers usually stayed on their 110-acre farm by the river near Little Falls, Minnesota.

As a child, Charles must have been unusually responsible because, at the age of six, he was given a .22 rifle by his grandfather. When Charles was eleven, his father taught him to drive a Model T. Charles never had an accident with either gun or car. In 1916 the Ford was replaced by a six-cylinder Saxon in which Charles—at the age of fourteen—not only decarbonized the engine but also changed the piston rings. He then drove the car, mostly over unpaved roads, more than 1,600 miles to California, with his mother and uncle as passengers. The trip took almost forty days.

Charles attended eleven schools—in Little Falls, Minneapolis, Dayton, Washington, and Rodondo Beach—and he hated them all. During the last two years of his schooling he ran his father's farm, and did it very well. Because the United States had entered World War I—in spite of Lindbergh, Sr.'s strenuous campaigning to keep her out—and food was urgently needed, Charles, Jr. was permitted to stay home from school to oversee food production on the farm.

At eighteen, Charles arrived at the University of Wisconsin on his motorbike. He wanted to study engineering, but had such a craving for flying—indeed, he had wanted to be a fighter pilot when the war was going on—that he left the university after two years in order to attend the Nebraska Aircraft Corporation, an aviation school in Lincoln, Nebraska. There, on April 9, 1922, after paying $500 to cover the complete course, Charles had his first flight in a Lincoln Standard biplane with his instructor, Otto Timm. This was not really a lesson, however, because the presence of a second flying enthusiast, Bud Gurney, in his cockpit meant the use of dual controls was impossible.* After eight

* Bud Gurney, who was two years younger than Charles, went on to complete a successful career as commercial pilot with United Airlines and as an engineer. When I met him at my Lindbergh lecture for the Los Angeles branch of the American Institute of Aeronautics & Astronautics (A.I.A.A.) in May, 1976, he invited me to fly the de Havilland Gypsy Moth he himself had reconstructed in Palo Alto. This plane is used by both Bud and his wife, Hilda, as a "fun" airplane, and for me, flying it—more than forty years since I had last flown my Moth *Rouge et Noir*—was as great a thrill as flying on the Concorde.

hours' instruction, Charles was ready to fly solo, but the company refused to allow that unless he could produce a bond to cover the plane in case he damaged it. Of course Charles did not have enough money for that. So off he went as an assistant to another pilot on a barnstorming tour in the South. (Barnstorming meant taking people aloft for brief flights over their towns for about five dollars per person.) But before the pilot took anyone up, he had to call attention to his flying machine. Charles's duties included wing-walking, which always attracted a crowd. While the plane was in flight, he would simply get up and take a little stroll along the wing, sometimes stopping to do a headstand! For this and other stunts, Charles wore a harness that secured him to the wing but was not visible to those watching his stunts from the ground. The wing-walker could stand on the wing while the plane made loops in the air. But wing-walking wasn't enough for Charles. He tried parachuting next. To everyone's amazement, Charles insisted on doing a "double drop" on his first jump. This stunt involved the use of two parachutes tied together with cord. After the first chute opened, the jumper would cut the cord binding the two together, thereby getting rid of the first one and relying on the second one to open and complete the fall.

In that first parachuting attempt, Charles was to drop 1,800 feet. The first chute opened quickly, but after he cut it loose, there was a long delay, during which he began to tumble head over heels. Eventually, the second parachute did open all right, and it turned out that the delay had occurred because a broken grocery-store string instead of sturdy cord had been used to bind the two chutes together. To the great relief of the spectators, Charles landed safely on a golf course just beyond the airfield.

In April, 1923, Charles bought his own Curtiss Jenny for

$500 at an auction of war-surplus planes. He had not flown for six months because he had had to work in the Robertson Aircraft Corporation plant in order to save enough money to buy his plane, but he managed to persuade one of the waiting pilots to give him a thirty-minute lesson in a plane with dual controls. The pilot instructed Charles and then suggested that he wait until the calm of evening for his first solo flight. Charles took the pilot's advice and, on April 9, patiently awaited the approach of dusk.

Going solo is one of the great events in a pilot's life, something he carries with him in his memory whatever else he may forget. In Charles's case, he completely missed out on that first tense moment when the instructor climbs out of the plane and says, "You're on your own!" Charles was already on his own. How utterly lonely he must have felt when he pushed open the throttle and the Curtiss Jenny began to bump its way faster and faster across the grass. There was no instructor's voice in his earphones, either to encourage or admonish him. The world below must have seemed to be standing still, holding its breath to see what would become of this lonely man in a flimsy machine clattering its way into the sky. Yet how well the plane seemed to perform, without the weight of an instructor on board. How ridiculously easy the whole idea of flying seemed to have become! Charles went around at about 1,000 feet, then headed for the downwind, or leeward, end of the field, turned to glide and correct for drift, and made a three-point landing—wheels and tailskid together—just as his instructor had shown him. How good that first solo landing felt!

Of all ordinary pilots, 99 percent make their first solo flights under the auspices of an instructor, but Charles took the entire responsibility on his own shoulders. After his first solo, he made a few more practice flights and then set off on his first cross-country flight: from Americus, Georgia, to Little Falls (via Texas), a distance of about 1,600 miles. Charles started this journey before his compass had been installed and, as a result, wandered 125 miles off course when he encountered stormy weather. After the inevitable forced landing, Charles realized that he could not go on without a dashboard compass, so during subsequent repairs, he fitted into place the one he had bought. On reaching home safely, he proceeded to fly his father around on an election campaign.

In order to enlarge his experience and fly more powerful airplanes, Charles applied for a flying cadetship, which would enable him to train with the Army Reserve. He passed his entrance exams and began training at Brooks Field, San Antonio, Texas, on March 15, 1924. Here, having previously flown trainers such as the Fokker, Curtiss Jenny, Hisso Standard, and an S.V.A. fighter, and having amassed 325 hours of flying time, Charles took to the air in a Curtiss Jenny, with the 90-h.p. Curtiss OX replaced by a 150-h.p. Hispano-Suiza. In addition, he flew the MB-3 and SE-5, single-engine fighters, a DH-4 bomber, a twin-engine Mitchell bomber, a TW-3 two-seater, and a Vought.

The most memorable incident of Charles's military training occurred when he was flying in an SE-5 formation of nine attacking a single DH-4 at 5,000 feet above the clouds. After making a dive on the "enemy," Charles felt a slight jolt as he pulled up over his target. The jolt was followed by a loud noise. His head was thrown against the cowling as his aircraft seemed to turn around and hang motionless. He was locked with another SE-5 and could see the pilot a few feet away to his left. The two planes, hopelessly enmeshed, started to mill around out of control with their wires screaming. The broken top wing kept striking Charles's head, as a

Charles Augustus Lindbergh at about twelve years, with his mongrel dog Dingo, on his father's farm at Little Falls, Minnesota
(Minnesota Historical Society)

Charles and his father (Lindbergh Papers, Yale)

Charles with his friend Bud Gurney in front of his barn-storming Hisso-Standard in 1923 at Lambert Field (John M. Noble, Lindbergh Papers, Yale)

Lindbergh in a Curtis Oriole at Lambert Field, St. Louis, in 1923 (John M. Noble, Lindbergh Papers, Yale)

Bud Gurney with the author after flying Gurney's de Havilland Gypsy Moth at Palo Alto in May, 1976 (John Grierson)

Charles's father, about 1923 (Minnesota Historical Society)

Evangeline Lindbergh prepares for a flight in her son's Canuck (Minnesota Historical Society)

Charles's parachute escape from the spinning Plywood Special at Lambert Field on June 2, 1924 (John M. Noble, Lindbergh Papers, Yale)

Charles after the landing in a strong wind that dislocated his shoulder, taken before his trip to the hospital in John Noble's Model T. The wreck of the airplane is in the background

(John M. Noble, Lindbergh Papers, Yale)

broken shutter strikes a window during a storm. Fortunately, both pilots were able to scramble out of their cockpits and make successful parachute drops. Charles was of course already skilled in parachuting, from his days as an exhibition and stunt flyer. He delayed his pull on the ripcord for several hundred feet so as to fall away first from the spinning wreckage. He just managed to miss some fifty-foot mesquite trees and slip himself into a plowed field. The only losses he noticed were his goggles, a vest-pocket camera, and the ripcord of his parachute.

All was not serious or dangerous at Brooks Field, however. High jinks and skylarking, fun and games, played a large part in life at all airfields in the 1920s. In a document he wrote to correct errors in Kenneth S. Davis's Lindbergh biography, *The Hero,* Charles had this to say:

> I enjoyed practical jokes, and took full part in playing them. I don't recall putting a frog or toad in anyone's bed, but it is possible that I did. . . . Practical jokes usually went with an environment that encouraged them, and they were seldom one-sided. When there was practical joking, everyone was usually having a lot of fun. . . . I tried to avoid playing any kind of a joke that might result in injury or, except where there was cause, unpleasantness that would be detrimental to personal relationships. . . .
>
> When I was a Flying Cadet at Brooks Field, I took the leading part in slipping a garden hose into the bunk of a sleeping cadet and turning the water full on. . . .
>
> I have, on a number of occasions, through the years, taken a leading part in dropping toothpaste into a snoring mouth. . . .
>
> A machine-shop trick was to wire tools etc. to a booster magneto so that anyone picking them up would get

a shock. I became expert at this. Mechanics were supposed to be alert enough to avoid getting caught, and when company officers or foremen came around, no one turned the magneto. . . .

I sometimes put explosive caps under toilet seats, so there would be a loud bang when anyone sat down (I learned how to do this from an Army colonel).

After receiving his Air Service Reserve wings, Charles went to St. Louis in order to find a job flying the mail. The Robertson Aircraft Corporation offered him the post of chief pilot to their line. While he waited for the Post Office contract to be awarded, Charles did some circus flying and some more barnstorming, during the course of which he landed in perilously small fields near isolated towns. In *The Spirit of St. Louis* he wrote of one of these towns where a colleague took up a flamboyant cowboy who had demanded a flight down the main street. While the colleague handled the controls, the man pulled out his revolver and proceeded to take pot shots at anything he saw on the street. When they landed, he proudly announced, "I shot this town up a'foot, an' I shot this town up a'hossback, an' now I shot this town up from a airplane!" Despite the risk of casualties, Charles and the other man waited to see if any more passengers would come.

Charles also had an assignment to test a new commercial plane, called a Plywood Special, built at Lambert Field in St. Louis. On the second test, Charles had difficulty in getting the machine to spin, but when he eventually got it going, he found it would not come out. At 1,500 feet, Charles realized the ground was getting rather close, so at 350 feet he bailed out, which left very little time for his chute to open; and even so, the plane was coming straight at him, and he was almost clobbered by it. There was a strong wind, which caused him to land heavily, and he was dragged. The result of this mishap was a dislocated shoulder and a ride to the hospital in a spectator's Model T. The owner of that Ford, John Noble, a keen amateur photographer and friend of Charles, recalls that even at this moment in history, Charles asked him not to let the press have his photographs of the damaged experimental plane because he was sure they would prejudice, quite unjustly, public opinion against the safety of flight.

At 5:30 A.M., on April 15, 1926, Charles took off on the inaugural airmail flight from Chicago to St. Louis, a journey of 250 miles, with intermediate landings at Peoria and Springfield, in a DH-4 especially converted for carrying mail. On this route, he and his two other pilots flew mostly at night, landing at the small, intermediate airports, with crude lighting and no radio, in all kinds of weather.

On September 16, when Charles was taking the mail north, he had an uneventful flight as far as Peoria, but then ran into darkness and fog that covered the countryside up to 600 feet. He attempted to turn back and fired a signal flare. But the flare failed to work, so he headed on again for Chicago. After an hour he saw a dull glow in the fog, which he hoped came from a town near Chicago. Several times he descended to the top of the murk, but on each descent downward vision was impossible. He circled for over half an hour and eventually climbed westward so as to keep away from Lake Michigan. At 1,500 feet, his engine cut, and he changed over to the reserve tank, which was good for twenty minutes. At the same time, he tried to open the mail compartment in order to throw out the sacks, but was unable to undo the latch. Just then, a light suddenly appeared through an opening in the fog, and he dived down toward it, success-

fully releasing his flare this time—the flare showed only un-
broken fog. So Charles climbed to 5,000 feet with his last
precious drops of gasoline and stepped overboard. The parachute opened well but, after Charles baled out, the plane's
engine picked up again and the aircraft began to chase him
down in a spiral, coming within 300 yards of hitting him.
But he landed, quite safely, in a cornfield.

The fourth time Charles's parachute saved his life was in
somewhat similar circumstances, except that darkness was
accompanied by snow. He climbed to 13,000 feet and, still
in cloud, reduced speed to 70 m.p.h.; with the machine on
an even keel, he stepped overboard. In falling snow, the descent was very cold, and the parachute started to oscillate.
The ground loomed suddenly, and Charles landed right on
top of a barbed-wire fence without even seeing it, but was
none the worse.

It was during one of Charles's mail flights on a moonlit
night that the idea of making a direct flight from North
America to Europe occurred to him. He had been thinking
about how his airline could improve its service by flying letters direct to New York instead of routing them north to
Chicago. This would require better aircraft than DH-4's
and Charles thought the new, long-range Bellanca with a
Whirlwind engine would be ideal for this purpose. He went
on from there to visualize how the Bellanca could even make
it possible to fly from New York to Paris in a single hop.
With 2,000 piloting hours to his credit, and confident that
the Atlantic weather could not possibly be worse than some
of the conditions he'd encountered on the night mail flights,
Charles felt that if he'd only had a Bellanca, he'd be off to
Paris.

His plan was now to seek financial backers and, with the
blessing of the Robertson Aircraft Corporation, he found

nine St. Louis businessmen willing to put up the high-risk capital of $15,000. Charles chipped in $2,000 of his own savings. In *The Spirit of St. Louis* he recounted that one banker who was reluctant to back an airplane with only one engine remarked, "Yes, you've only got a life to lose, Slim. But don't forget, I've got a reputation to lose." Nevertheless, this same man ended by giving Charles open-ended support.

The Bellanca was initially in the control of the Wright Company and then of Charles Levine. Charles had traveled three times to New York and had virtually clinched the deal, when Levine suddenly made it a condition of sale that he alone would provide the crew for the Atlantic flight, so the whole thing fell through. Fortunately, Charles had also contacted Ryan Airlines in San Diego. Ryan agreed to build in sixty days a special high-wing monoplane with a Whirlwind engine for the Paris flight, at a cost of $10,580. Special equipment would cost extra.

Since the distance to Paris from New York was given as 3,600 miles and westerly winds were expected throughout the flight, it seemed that a range of 4,040 miles would be adequate at a cruising speed of 75-110 m.p.h. For this purpose, an enormous fuselage fuel tank was mounted directly in front of the cockpit, leaving Charles nothing but vision through side windows and the transparent roof. The power plant was the latest Wright Whirlwind J5C nine-cylinder radial of 220 h.p., which had a great reputation for reliability.

Charles planned the flight meticulously in every detail. Radio was out because of its weight and unreliability, and so was the use of a sextant because he thought it would be impossible to hold an absolutely steady course and take sights simultaneously. He would rely entirely on dead reckoning and hope to be able to obtain sufficient sightings of the ocean to calculate wind speed and direction from the waves. The route was divided into 100-mile sectors, and Charles planned to alter course every hour so as to take into account the great-circle track and changes of magnetic variation. A great circle is a plane cutting through a sphere, in this case the earth; thus a great circle is the shortest distance between any two points on the earth's surface. Magnetic variation is the amount in degrees by which the heading of the magnetic north shown by the compass varies east or west from that of true north at any given point on the earth's surface, related to a particular year.

Charles arrived at the Ryan factory in San Diego on February 23, 1927, determined to stay with the company throughout his airplane's manufacture. In addition to the desirability of seeing the job through, Charles wanted to keep the company up on all the news, so that he could lead the field for the $25,000 Raymond Orteig Prize with the first flight from New York to Paris, or vice versa. The prize money had been sitting in a bank since 1919, when the offer was first made. Charles knew that Levine was likely to put the Bellanca into the running, that Lieutenant Commander Noel Davis was preparing a stripped-down three-engine Huff-Daland bomber, and that Admiral Richard Byrd had his trimotor Fokker, which he was repairing after a takeoff crash, and that in France Captains Charles Nungesser and François Coli were preparing their Levasseur, *Oiseau Blanc*. Another would-be contestant had been Major René Fonck, but he had already crashed and burned up his trimotor Sikorsky while trying to take off from New York the previous September 21; Fonck and his copilot were unhurt in the crash, but two crew members were burned to death. It looked as though the Bellanca should easily be first on the starting line, but dissension and quarrels about who should be in the crew were a major stumbling block.

The designer and men in the crude little workshops at

Ryan worked around the clock. There was the spark of competitive spirit in the air, and the men realized how pressing it was to get their ship onto the starting line before any other.

Navigation instruments on board consisted of a drift sight (which Charles never used), a turn-and-slip gyro, an earth-inductor compass, and an ordinary magnetic compass. When the mechanics were installing the magnetic compass, they decided that the only satisfactory place for it was in the middle of the roof. But that meant that a mirror on the dashboard would be necessary so that the pilot would be able to read the instrument. There was no satisfactory mirror in the hangar, but a young spectator offered the circular mirror from her powder compact. The ideal size, it was gratefully accepted and stuck on the dashboard—with chewing gum! The fuel system of five tanks was controlled by a battery of fourteen cocks. There was a knob on the dashboard that enabled the periscope to be extended out of the left side of the fuselage, and retracted when not in use.

While mechanics, designers, and others worked on the plane, Charles made good use of his time, spending some of it on navigation charts. He never wandered far from the factory until the magic day of the first flight, April 28.

He was pleased with the quick takeoff (at light-load, of course) and the easy climb. The controls, however, were not particularly good—for example, the ailerons had been made short and not very responsive in order to avoid overstraining the extended wings—and stability, as predicted, was marginal. This might have been improved by using larger tail surfaces, but that would have involved extra weight and a delay, which Charles preferred to do without. He would accept the consequences. The indicated top speed was 128 m.p.h. at low altitude, which was 3.5 m.p.h. better than had been estimated.

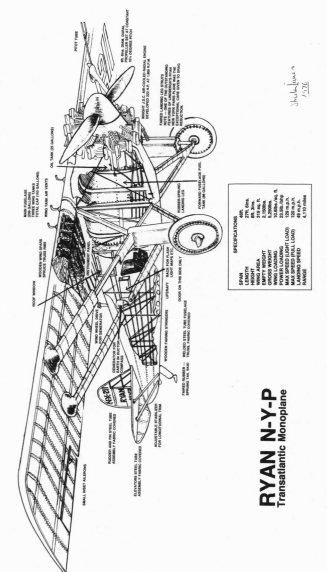

RYAN N-Y-P
Transatlantic Monoplane

SMALL INSET AILERONS

RUDDER AND FIN STEEL TUBE
ASSEMBLY, FABRIC COVERED

ELEVATORS STEEL TUBE
ASSEMBLY, FABRIC COVERED

FAIRED RUBBER —
SPRING TAIL SKID

ADJUSTABLE STABILIZER
FOR LONGITUDINAL TRIM

WELDED STEEL TUBE FUSELAGE
TRUSS, FABRIC COVERED

WOODEN FAIRING STRINGERS

GENERATOR FOR
EARTH IN DUCTOR
COMPASS

WIND WHEEL DRIVE
FOR GENERATOR

LIFERAFT

DOOR ON THIS SIDE ONLY

RACK FOR FLASH
LIGHT MAPS ETC.

ROOF WINDOW

INSTRUMENT PANEL

WOODEN WING SPARS
SPRUCE TRUSS RIBS

MAIN FUSELAGE
(209 GALLONS)
THREE WING TANKS
TOTAL CAP (103 GALLONS)

WING TANK AIR VENTS

OIL TANK (25 GALLONS)

RUBBER-SPRING
LANDING LEG

FORWARD FUSELAGE FUEL
TANK (88 GALLONS)

PITOT TUBE

8ft, 9ins. DIAM. DURAL
PROPELLER SET AT CONSTANT
16¼ DEGREE PITCH

WRIGHT J.5.C. AIR-COOLED RADIAL ENGINE
DEVELOPED 223 H.P. AT 1,800 R.P.M.

FAIRED LANDING LEG STRUTS
NOTE — ONE OF THE OUTSTANDING
FEATURES OF LINDBERGH'S RYAN
NEW YORK PARIS PLANE WAS THE
EXCEPTIONAL CARE GIVEN TO DRAG
REDUCTION.

SPECIFICATIONS

SPAN	46ft.
LENGTH	27ft. 6ins.
HEIGHT	8ft. 3ins.
WING AREA	319 sq. ft.
EMPTY WEIGHT	2,150lbs.
GROSS WEIGHT	5,250lbs.
WING LOADING	16.6lbs./sq. ft.
POWER LOADING	23.5lb./bhp
MAX SPEED (LIGHT LOAD)	129 m.p.h.
MAX SPEED (FULL LOAD)	120 m.p.h.
LANDING SPEED	49 m.p.h.
RANGE	4,110 miles

NX-211
RYAN

Spirit of St. Louis. The aircraft now hangs in the Smithsonian Institution (Sheila Innes)

After running thorough speed and load tests for over a week, Charles was ready to fly East. On the afternoon of May 10, he set off for St. Louis. By dusk he was crossing the canyons and cliffs of Arizona and went on climbing to 8,000 feet. There was an almost full moon, but haze reduced visibility over the rugged contours below. He had reached the foothills of the Rockies when suddenly the engine began to miss and run rough. All that could be seen below looked hostile and barren—a most unpromising prospect for a forced landing with 200 gallons still on board. Charles tried working the throttle back and forth and then the mixture control, but they were no good. So little power was coming from the vibrating engine that height was being lost fairly quickly at first, and the need for doing the best possible crash landing seemed inevitable. However, in spite of its roughness, the Whirlwind began to put out more power and slow the rate of descent. Progressively, the engine vibrated less and held the airplane up better until, at 7,000 feet, Charles found he had leveled off. He could not imagine what on earth had caused the trouble. Then, by again pumping the throttle and mixture control back and forth, he managed to clear the irregular running and realized he had almost certainly been suffering carburetor icing.

After this experience, he wanted as much space as possible between himself and the mountains and climbed to 13,000 feet. However, he had no more trouble and reached Lambert Field, St. Louis, 14 hours, 25 minutes after takeoff. With typical Lindbergh lack of ceremony, he had had SPIRIT OF ST. LOUIS painted on his Ryan when it was built at San Diego, and now the name made him doubly welcome at Lambert Field, where all his backers could see and acclaim the product of their enterprise. After an enthusiastic welcome, Charles hurried on, on May 12, to Curtiss Field, Long Island, New York.

In New York, the final touches to prepare Charles's *Spirit of St. Louis* for the great trip were made. These included such items as a heater for the carburetor air intake (controlled by a lever beside the throttle) and a new earth-inductor compass. Although the press was everywhere and began to call Charles the "Flying Fool," reporters could not help but be impressed by the fact that he was the only Atlantic challenger to have flown his airplane 2,500 miles from the West Coast, which was further than the actual ocean hop, in 21 hours, 45 minutes, via St. Louis.

Admiral Byrd visited Lindbergh's hangar and very kindly offered him the use of the airport next door, Roosevelt Field. Byrd had a lease on it and had built a special 5,000-foot grass runway there for his trimotor Fokker, which had almost completed its tests. Other callers were Giuseppe Bellanca and Clarence Chamberlin, René Fonck and Tony Fokker, Chance Vought, and Harry Guggenheim (a millionaire who was interested in promoting aviation). There was obviously a good spirit of comradeship among the competitors for the Raymond Orteig Prize.

By May 16, the *Spirit of St. Louis* had finished all its test flights and was absolutely ready, but the weather forecast for over the Atlantic was bad for some days ahead. Charles walked over from his hangar to Roosevelt Field to make a detailed inspection. It had the advantage of being longer than any other airstrip in the New York area, but he found the runway rather narrow and soft. Would it be firm enough to insure proper takeoff speed of an overloaded plane? Charles knew that if he did not take off successfully, he would probably be burned to death.

Chapter II ➤ THE FLIGHT

On May 19, James H. ("Doc") Kimball of the Weather Bureau forecast continuing bad weather over the Atlantic for at least twenty-four hours, and Charles resigned himself to not being able to start the next day. Dick Blythe, a Wright representative, therefore arranged to take Charles to New York City to see *Rio Rita*, the hit musical show of the day. The outing would include a backstage visit, and the two were joined by Franklin Mahoney, president of Ryan Aircraft Corporation. On the way into town, one of the group suggested making a call to Kimball, just to see if there had been a change in the weather. Charles immediately agreed, and Blythe went to phone the Weather Bureau. He came back beaming. His news was amazing—there had just been a sudden let-up in the bad weather. Conditions were improving, although they would still be bad on parts of the route for a day or two. There was just a chance that the clearance in New York would allow a dawn takeoff.

Determined not to be forestalled by Byrd or Chamberlin, Charles now planned to have a hundred gallons of fuel put

on board just before ferrying the *Spirit of St. Louis* to
Roosevelt Field at dawn or as soon as the drizzle eased and
the clouds had lifted. The rest of the fuel would go in at the
field.

Now Charles's main preoccupation was how much sleep
he could get before takeoff. En route to the airfield, the
party had a quick meal at the Queensboro Plaza, and
Charles remembered that they must get the National Aero-
nautic Association representative to place the sealed barograph—without which the flight could not be considered "official"—on board before dawn, and that was arranged. At
Curtiss Field, there was a welcome lack of activity at the
Byrd and Chamberlin hangars. It seemed that the others
wanted confirmation of the forecast improvement before attempting to start.

On returning to his hotel, Charles found that word had already leaked out about his intended takeoff. Reporters and
autograph hunters were swarming in the lobby. It was nearly
midnight before he reached his room, leaving only two and
a half hours for sleep. A friend was set on guard outside
Charles's door to ward off uninvited guests.

Charles recounted in his book *The Spirit of St. Louis* that
he was about to doze off when there was a hammering on
his door. It was, incredibly, the man put there to keep people out! Charles could not imagine what dire emergency with
his plane or the weather could have caused this intrusion,
when the man blurted out, "Slim, what am I going to do
when you're gone?" Charles replied, "I don't know. There
are plenty of other problems to solve before we have to think
about that one." This rude awakening ended the desire to
sleep—anyway, only two hours were left—and Charles simply turned over and over in his mind the prospects of his
flight: how much fuel he should carry now that the tanks had

been found to be twenty-five gallons bigger in capacity than the design, what his competitors were doing, the unfairness of the sixty-day rule* stipulated for the Orteig Prize, and so on. Consequently, Charles never had any sleep, and by 2:30 A.M., he was out of bed and dressed. Snatching a very light breakfast before leaving the hotel, he was driven to the air-field by Frank Tichenor, publisher of *Aero Digest*. The weather was gloomy, and low clouds and drizzle ruled out any possibility of flying yet. Byrd, it was rumored, had to fly some more tests, and the Bellanca was apparently held up by a court injunction. So, if only the weather picked up and the ground were not too soggy, it looked as if Charles could show them both a clean pair of heels. A message from the Weather Bureau reaffirmed the likelihood of the fog lifting between New York and Newfoundland.

In view of the present unflyability of the weather, Charles decided to save time by having his plane towed, with the tailskid lashed to the back of a truck, to adjacent Roosevelt Field instead of waiting to fly it across. It was an awkward tow and had to proceed, even with a police escort, at a snail's pace through the gloom and incessant rain. It was, as Charles later wrote in *The Spirit of St. Louis*, "more like a funeral procession than the beginning of a flight to Paris."

At daybreak, the weather was a little better; although perhaps there was a slight lightening of the clouds, they certainly were not high enough to allow a takeoff. The wind was light and variable, making it difficult to decide which end of the runway would be best for the start. Because hangars and houses were at the western end of the runway and only telephone wires at the eastern end, Charles favored

---

* This required that there be a minimum interval of sixty days between the acceptance date of any competitor and the completion of his flight date.

a start from west to east and had his plane positioned accordingly before putting the full 450 gallons on board, which made the total weight 5,250 pounds.

Just after 7:30 A.M., there was a definite improvement as the drizzle stopped and clouds lifted, so Charles made the fateful decision to go aboard. The engine did not seem to be giving full power, but the mechanics assured Charles that this was due only to the low barometric pressure. Surface conditions were far from perfect, with mud everywhere and water lying in pools on the runway as far as one could see toward the telephone wires and misty horizon. What little wind there was just then seemed to be blowing from the west, making it a tail wind on the runway.

This was going to be what was described in pilots' jargon as the sort of takeoff timed with a tear-off calendar rather than with a stop-watch. Everything seemed to be less favorable than when the load tests were flown at Camp Kearney: the ground was soft instead of hard; the wind was blowing from slightly behind; and now the *Spirit of St. Louis* had to lift another 1,000 pounds under such adverse conditions. Yet Charles was convinced that, in spite of everything, he would get off the ground.

Although the mechanics had even rubbed grease on the tires to try and prevent the mud from sticking to them, when Charles sat in the cockpit and opened up to full throttle, the plane barely moved: he was literally stuck in the mud. Some of the spectators ran toward the plane and started pushing on the struts so hard that Lindbergh was afraid they would buckle. At this rate, he wondered how on earth, with the engine roaring, he would ever reach flying speed. But the efforts of the bystanders were helpful and had him going first at a walking pace and then as fast as they could run, until the *Spirit of St. Louis* drew ahead at last.

Keeping straight with the tail down was proving difficult because it was taking so long to gain enough speed for the rudder to bite. After the first thousand feet, the controls were just beginning to have a tiny bit of feel about them and in a few seconds more, the tail started to lift—a very welcome sign. At the halfway mark, the engine was beginning to hum as it picked up revs; now, with increasing speed, the need for keeping accurately to Byrd's narrow runway was greater than ever. The point of no return had come—Charles had his last chance to abandon the run and had to commit himself to carrying on regardless of the consequences. Just to convince himself that he was winning, he gave the stick a pull and, sure enough, he staggered into the air, but only for a moment, until his overloaded craft fell back onto the ground. The undercarriage was taking a terrible hammering, though the fact that there were only 2,000 feet to go meant that now nothing but flight would prevent absolute disaster. Another hop into the air, a wing drop, and a mighty splash—and the *Spirit of St. Louis* fell back into a pool. Again he left the ground with the same result. But he took one more long hop and—at last—with a final bound, the *Spirit of St. Louis* was airborne. Charles kept the nose down in order to gain full flying speed and started a gentle climb, which just cleared the telephone wires by twenty feet.

Now he had triumphed over the first and one of the greatest obstacles of his flight as he made his way above Long Island at 200 feet. Soon the rain stopped altogether, the mist and clouds eased, and a tail wind was blowing. Thus Fortune smiled radiantly on the start of this historic flight.

As Charles passed Cape Cod, he set out on the first major sea crossing of his flying career: 250 miles to Nova Scotia. Because he believed that there would be a performance advantage in flying extremely low so as to stay inside the boundary layer (the layer of air close to the surface), he kept at between 20 and 100 feet above the waves. This of course called for greater precision in order to avoid getting dumped into the sea. After only three hours he began to feel cramped and tired and had his first sip of water. In the fifth hour he hit land and was barely six miles off course—an acceptable result—and he worked out that it would be equivalent to hitting Ireland within fifty miles of the aiming point; he would be well satisfied with that. So far the weather had been good, but soon dark clouds appeared over the land as sudden gusts buffeted the *Spirit of St. Louis*. In his still-overloaded state after five hours' flying, Charles worried about the flexing of the wings and wondered how long they would stand up to this violent treatment. He reduced speed in the face of increasing turbulence, as squall after squall struck, lightning lit up the rocks and trees below, and the rain poured down. He carefully watched the direction of the blustery wind, oscillating with the squalls between northwest and southwest. At last it swung to south and finally to southeast when it began to die, as a sure indication that the storm had almost passed, and two hours later, when he cleared Cape Breton Island, having been thrown east of his planned track, the sun was shining brilliantly and visibility was unlimited.

About this time Charles seriously considered fixing the windows in their frames so as to reduce the draft and to improve performance by the better streamlining. But on reflection he decided that the draft was so important for keeping himself awake, he must have it and forgo whatever gain there would be in speed through having the windows installed.

Over the Atlantic again he found the urge to sleep was almost overwhelming. "If I could throw myself down on a bed," he wrote in *The Spirit of St. Louis*, "I'd be asleep in an instant. In fact, if I didn't know the result, I'd fall asleep just as I am, sitting up in the cockpit—I'm beyond the stage where I need a bed, or even to lie down. My eyes feel dry and hard as stones. The lids pull down with pounds of weight against their muscles." Then, after shaking his head and body roughly, flexing the muscles of his arms and legs, and stamping his feet on the floorboards, he went on: "The worst part about fighting sleep is that the harder you fight the more you strengthen your enemy, and the more you weaken your resistance to him." Paris was still 2,800 miles away, and with a whole night to fly through, he was conscious of already making many involuntary course alterations due to his tiredness.

A sudden and unexpected change in the ocean from open water to a dazzling ice field hit Charles like a bucket of cold water—a fascinating stimulant which, added to the instability of his machine, helped to keep him awake. Besides, he had to exercise his mind by periodically checking his navigation, taking instrument readings, and realigning his fuel tanks as necessary at hourly intervals.

Just before the islands of Miquelon and Saint Pierre heralded Newfoundland, the ice changed to open water, and Charles reached St. John's only 11 hours, 15 minutes out of New York, his indicated cruising speed having ranged from 94 to 107 m.p.h., which gave him an overall average of almost exactly 101 m.p.h. for the 1,137 miles. Now he was over the very spot where, almost eight years before, John Alcock and Arthur Whitten Brown had taken off in their twin-engine Vickers Vimy from a field 400 yards long on the first direct Atlantic flight. They had some exciting times; once, after two hours, when one of their exhaust pipes melted and fell off, it allowed a flame to impinge on a flying wire and make it red-hot. If the tail wind had not almost equaled their cruising speed of 65 m.p.h., it would have been wise to turn back, but because of that wind turning back was im-

possible. Later, they got into a spin in a cloud and finally
ended in a bog at Clifden in County Galway, Ireland.

Charles was routing himself over St. John's (although it
meant that he would be 90 miles south of his originally
planned great circle) for convenience due to his having been
pushed southward by bad weather and because he thought
it would be good to be seen and "clocked out" at the start
of the most dangerous part of his flight, the 1,887-mile leg
to Ireland. He therefore made one straight dive over the center of the town in order to be sure that the *Spirit of St. Louis*
would not pass overhead unseen.

A sense of exhilaration filled the lone flier as he pointed
the *Spirit of St. Louis* out over the mighty Atlantic, heading
into the gathering dusk. From the waves he gauged the wind
at 30 knots on his tail, and in the fading light scattered icebergs presented themselves as large, eerie monsters, glisten-
ing in their dazzling whiteness. Fog lay below on the water,
and at first the icebergs showed through, but the fog built up
in a solid mass so that Charles was forced to climb to keep
above it, until after two hours he had been driven up to
9,300 feet. In the darkness—for there was no moon as yet—
he reflected that the going had been almost too easy so far.
"A victory given stands pale beside a victory won," he later
wrote in *The Spirit of St. Louis*. "A pilot has the right to
choose his battlefield—that is the strategy of flight. But once
that battlefield is attained, conflict should be welcomed, not
avoided. If a pilot fears to test his skill with the elements, he
has chosen the wrong profession."

At first, half a dozen bright stars pierced the overcast
sky, but soon the haze thickened until it was as dense as
cloud, and Charles noted regretfully that the *Spirit of St.
Louis* was too unstable to fly well on instruments. He turned
over in his mind the question of how high he would be pre-

pared to climb in order to keep above the gathering clouds of the storm area ahead and tentatively decided on 15,000 feet, no higher. He realized that in going even as high as that he would risk lowering his efficiency through lack of oxygen and make it still more difficult to stay awake; perhaps that is why he never went above 10,500 feet, contenting himself with threading his way through the high valleys of turbulent cumulus.

As he gazed at the myriad stars all around, his mind turned to religion, to the infinite magnitude of the universe and the utter insignificance of man. He recorded his thoughts in *The Spirit of St. Louis*: "And man conscious of it all—a worldly audience to what if not to God?"

At 10,000 feet, for the first time, Charles noticed the cold and zipped up his flight suit. He thought he would fly blind without climbing any more because the clouds seemed to tower so far above him. The turbulence in these clouds was severe, making the control of the plane really hard work. What was worse was that when he flashed his light on the struts, he saw that they were glazed with ice. It was bad enough to have ice on the struts, but it was more damaging to have ice on the wings and even worse on the pitot-head (the open tube facing into the air stream that leads the air into the air-speed indicator). If that became clogged with ice, blind-flying would be virtually impossible. So Charles had to fly out of the cloud as quickly as he could and regain the clear atmosphere somehow, before the air-speed indicator iced up. As he turned, the air speed kept dropping, and he could not tell whether the indicator was telling the truth or was simply clogged with ice. Now he pushed the engine to full throttle and, with stick forward, was relieved to see the air speed coming back. All the same, the ice was increasing rapidly, and he badly needed a way out of the cloud.

Somehow, Charles edged the plane around without stalling, straightened up, and determined to hold out for the three minutes it would take him to break out. It seemed an eternity, waiting with such a dangerous build-up of ice. What a relief it was when, dimly at first in the haze, Charles caught a glimpse of the stars. The ice, of course was still there, deforming the leading edge of the wing and adding its unwelcome weight, but the air-speed indicator was reading only 5 m.p.h. below normal, which was not serious. Now the need to weave a path between the towering mountains of cloud was greater than ever, so as to avoid any increase of ice by touching them or the disorienting effects of turbulence on entering them.

For the first time, Charles seriously considered turning back, but it would have been a pretty hard job to find his way through the maze of hazy passageways he had already penetrated. Over fourteen hours had passed since he had left New York, and when he noticed that the ice on the wings seemed to be completely gone, his mind was made up to continue.

At this point, the two compasses began to behave oddly, the main one rocking through 60° and even 90° at times, the earth-inductor all over the place, so that Charles thought he must be in a magnetic storm. It was only the fact that stars were visible in the black darkness that enabled him to keep his plane pointed in an easterly direction. In the midst of all these worries, the young pilot again began to feel terribly sleepy, and it was lucky that the moon started to rise, illuminating the clouds and providing a distraction. Yet far ahead, moonlight revealed a higher cloud formation, which seemed to block the way east! Once again, the question of turning back raced through Charles's mind, and once more he rejected it.

Navigation had suffered from the many alterations of course due to the cloudiness and the peculiar behavior of the compasses, and on top of it all Charles worried that he had been 90 miles south of the great circle in order to pass over St. John's. His drowsiness was beginning to affect his usual aim for perfection. He later recounted in his book *The Spirit of St. Louis*, ". . . why should I worry about a trivial five or ten degrees [off course]? Ten degrees isn't much of an angle – – – I can't possibly miss the whole continent of Europe." He diverted the slipstream into his face and, of this, he later wrote, "I let my eyelids fall shut for five seconds; then raise them against tons of weight. Protesting, they won't open wide until I force them with my thumb, and lift the muscles of my forehead to help keep them in place." The *Spirit of St. Louis* refused to be left unattended for five seconds—such was her instability.

Feeling the cold, Charles really wanted to put on his flying boots but decided that it would upset his course-keeping so much that it was not worth while, and he preferred to stay cold. Again he thought of fitting in the windows in order to reduce the draft, but again he decided to keep the draft as a safeguard against falling asleep.

He tried to spread out his charts enough to read them by flashlight in the cramped cockpit and found that doing so made him wander all over the sky. After several attempts, causing him to yaw and bank drunkenly, he gave it up and decided to try to memorize the outline of Europe relative to his flight. He felt he must have been pushed south of course, first by the storms in Nova Scotia, then by running south of the great circle to hit St. John's, and finally by southward deviations to avoid the thunderheads. And on top of that, the wind above the clouds could have blown him southward too.

Suddenly the lights of a ship seemed to appear, suggesting that the belt of sea fog had broken, but then the lights continued to rise, and Charles realized it was stars he was looking at as he dropped his right wing to level off.

After this, things began to improve: the compasses became steadier, the haze was gone, along with the wing ice, and the clouds were dispersing. Even so, having flown more than five hours out of sight of the surface, Charles was worried about where the winds might have carried him. As for his own physical feelings, he later wrote in *The Spirit of St. Louis*, "My body requires no attention. It's not hungry. It's neither warm nor cold." He even wished that he had left his body behind at Long Island or St. Louis and done the flight without it!

Six hours out from St. John's brought the dawn, and Charles recorded, "With this faint trace of day, the uncontrollable desire to sleep falls over me in quilted layers. . . . This is the hour I've been dreading; the hour against which I've tried to steel myself. I know it's the beginning of my greatest test. This will be the worst time of all, this early hour of the second morning—the third morning, it is, since I've slept."

His back was stiff, his shoulders ached, his face burned, and his eyes smarted: all he wanted was the forbidden sleep. The plane had gone 10° off course, and Charles bounced himself up and down as he ruddered his machine back onto the right heading—and almost immediately it went off again. In trying to shake himself into wakefulness, he kept repeating, "There's no alternative but death and failure. *No alternative but death and failure.*" As full daylight came, the urge to sleep lessened slightly, and he managed to keep a better course, refreshed by a sip of water. Because Charles had had nothing to eat since breakfast the previous day, he thought about eating one of the five sandwiches that lay in a grease-spotted bag, but he feared that eating might make him feel sleepier, so he continued his fast.

Fortunately, the earth-inductor compass had regained its sanity; Charles knew that if he failed to keep the instruments in balance, loss of control and disaster would quickly follow. Occasionally, the cloud would break, but there was a mixture of layered stratus and towering cumulus all around, which never relieved him from instrument-flying for long.

At the nineteenth hour Charles was beginning to lose interest in his hourly log and managed to make himself record little more than the fact that he was at 9,000 feet and, by estimate, halfway to Paris. He thought at first that might be an occasion for celebrating by eating a sandwich, but he simply did not want food or water, nor did he bother to make his hourly change of course because he felt it was too much effort. "But what difference do two or three degrees make when I'm letting the nose swing several times that much to one side or the other of my heading?" he wrote in *The Spirit of St. Louis.*

Although he had not changed altitude when he exercised his "thermometer," which consisted of sticking a finger out into the slipstream to see whether it felt just cold, very cold, or quite horrible, he was sure the air was warmer and well above freezing. Clouds again covered the sea and presented a solid wall through which he had to make his way on instruments at 9,000 feet.

At the beginning of the twentieth hour out of New York, Charles made his last serious effort to keep a log and then began to descend, for he had been unable to see the waves for a wind check for over seven hours. With no knowledge of any change in the barometric pressure, he could not rely on his altimeter-reading as he went down, so he decided to limit his descent to 1,000 feet. Suddenly, at 8,000 feet, he saw a deep funnel between pillars of cloud with a heavy sea running on the ocean at the bottom. Anxious not to lose contact he forced the *Spirit of St. Louis* down until she was diving at 140 m.p.h. with engine throttled back. He had to spiral around the funnel so as not to lose it, descending at such a rate that his ears began to pop. At 2,000 feet he was under the lowest cloud layer, having lost his sense of direction, but when he had regained his course, he saw that he had a quartering tail wind from the northwest, which must have been driving him ahead but also south of course.

Now he went down to 50 feet above the huge breaking waves and reckoned that the wind speed was up to 60 m.p.h., for the spray was being blown off the whitecaps like rain. He did not fancy his chances of surviving a forced landing in such a sea, even with a dinghy aboard. His greatest worry: what had been his past errors in navigation when he had had to alter course so often to avoid the weather, with no idea where the wind was carrying him from hour to hour?

He felt, without any real proof, that he might be so far south he was in danger of striking the Bay of Biscay. Before he could decide what to do, fog covered the sea, forcing him to climb, and he was pitched about all over the sky. At 1,000 feet he leveled off and proceeded to fly blind, having his work cut out just to keep on an even keel.

After nearly an hour the nose went down without warning, and one wing dropped as he dived toward the waves; Charles had, in his own words, "been asleep with open eyes." Quickly coming to his senses, he applied stick and rudder, intending to correct the dive and get back into level flight. But the pointer of the turn indicator went hard to port and the air speed dropped, indicating a steep climbing turn from where he had just been diving, for he was beginning to lose control. The impact of this knowledge acted like an electric shock: he started to set the instruments into place slowly and deliberately. He did regain a level course, though he felt as if he were flying in a dream and his conscious mind had ceased to work.

Suddenly he realized that the nose had again gone up and slewed 16° off course. Once he had put that right, things seemed to get better, and he climbed to 1,500 feet so as to reduce the risk of crashing into the water because of sleep.

At the start of the twenty-first hour, Charles took no readings for his log—he felt he needed all his energy to control the plane, for he had been flying on instruments for almost nine hours and thought he was becoming hypnotized by them. He kept having the sensation of falling asleep and waking up seconds later.

In spite of the precarious balance between wakefulness and sleep, Charles once more went down to investigate what he thought was a clearing in the fog as the mist lightened and darkened alternately, but he found no real opening even though he went so low that he was in salt spray whipped off whitecaps by the wind, and clipping five feet above the breakers with his wheels. Frustrated in his attempt, he went back up to 1,000 feet. But in a few minutes breaks started to open up, accompanied by rain.

Before a real break had arrived, he became aware of ghostly presences in his fuselage, as though a host of vaguely outlined forms with friendly human voices had come aboard. This extraordinary phenomenon did not seem to worry him, though he confessed later, in *The Spirit of St. Louis*, "I'm on the border line of life and a greater realm beyond, as though caught in the field of gravitation between two planets. . . . Am I crossing the bridge which one sees only in last, departing moments? Am I already beyond the point from which I can bring my vision back to earth and men? Death no longer seems the final end it used to be, but rather the entrance to a new and free existence which includes all space, all time."

Not until the end of the twenty-second hour was the main storm area passed—though the fringe effects lasted half an hour more—when Charles was faced with a new kind of phenomenon: a coastline with hills and clumps of trees in mid-Atlantic. This made him wonder whether he was fast asleep, or had flown north to Greenland, or had become completely disoriented. How could there be land in mid-Atlantic? An island lay straight across his course but just as he reached it, the shades of gray and white and purple disappeared. The fog mirage was over, and now the horizon became bright and sharp. He later wrote in *The Spirit of St. Louis*, "I'm capable only of holding my plane aloft, and laxly pointed toward a heading I set some hours ago. No extra energy remains. I'm as strengthless as the vapor limbs of the spirits to whom I listen."

A couple of times he even struck his face sharply with his fist as hard as he could to stimulate his body, but he felt no pain. How on earth could he keep himself awake? "The alternative is death and failure!" he muttered again, and for the first time Charles doubted his ability to endure. He tried every kind of exercise possible in the cockpit and turned his face into the slipstream in a final effort to keep awake. Gradually, somehow, his strength came back. He wrote in *The Spirit of St. Louis*, "I've been hanging over the chasm of eternity, holding onto the ledge with my fingertips; but now I'm gaining strength, I'm crawling upward. Consciousness is coming back." And so he began his twenty-fifth hour.

He thought of taking readings with the drift sight, which lay in a rack behind his chair and had never been brought out. But it seemed that it would be just as difficult to take drift readings as to operate a sextant and hold a steady course, which had been abandoned as impossible. He therefore decided to leave the drift sight untouched and carry on judging wind strength and direction simply by looking at the waves through the window. Now he was feeling hot enough to make him unzip his flying suit and cup his hand into the slipstream to bring a draft against his face.

On considering all possible errors due to course alterations, weather, and wind factors, he concluded that his maximum possible error would be 440 miles south, which would put him on the Biscay coast after dark, or 425 miles north, which would make him hit the Hebrides. He really wanted to cross whatever coast he met in daylight so as to be able to pinpoint his position and start map-reading. Fortunately, he decided to ignore these extremes and carry on a heading of 115°, which paralleled the wind streaks driven on by a westerly wind at about 30 m.p.h. in bright sunlight.

It was during the twenty-sixth hour that Charles reached into the pocket of his flight suit for a fresh handkerchief and was amazed to discover with it a little medallion. It was, he assumed, a silver St. Christopher's medal of Saint and Child from an absolutely unknown donor.* Maybe it came from a

---

* The medal was actually of Our Lady of Loreto, the patron of aviators, and was given to Charles by Father Henry Hussman, to whom Charles used to give flying lessons. The legend of Our Lady of Loreto is that angels carried the Virgin's house from Jerusalem when it was threatened with destruction by the Turks in 1291 and made a simulated forced landing on a hill in Fersalto in Dalmatia, where it remained for three years. It was then flown over to Loreto, near Ancona, Italy. Thus through entirely different circumstances, Charles and I, who were both Protestants, both carried medallions of Our Lady of Loreto for our Atlantic flights, I through being given one, duly blessed, by the Irish wife of the British Minister when I flew through Bucharest, Rumania, in mid-winter 1934, and Charles unknowingly by Father Hussman. The medallion seemed to have been lost at the end of the flight, but the Jefferson Memorial Building in St. Louis, which now houses all of Charles's decorations and trophies on behalf of the Missouri Historical Society, has traced the medallion to a St. Louis citizen who holds it.

man, he thought, maybe a woman, maybe young or maybe old, from a person who asked no thanks but simply sent it with a silent blessing or a prayer. What a dramatic discovery to make way out over a watery wilderness!

At the end of the twenty-sixth hour, Charles thought he saw a large fish, the first living thing since Newfoundland. He thought perhaps it was a porpoise breaking the surface of the sea, and the sight revived him with a new interest. It intrigued him to think that although the ocean itself was certain death for him, for other creatures it meant life.

Charles realized that he was constantly ruddering the plane to the left because instinctively he believed he was south of course due to his departure at St. John's, but he felt relieved as the wind decreased and only cumulus clouds lay scattered ahead with dim squalls in the distance.

Now that the sun was shining, Charles tried on a pair of sunglasses given him by a Long Island doctor, but the glasses made the sky look overcast again, and their comfort only increased his desire to sleep, so he had to remove them. He also tried breaking a capsule of smelling salts, taken from the doctor's first-aid kit, and found his senses had become so dulled that he could smell absolutely nothing.

In trying to stimulate his mind, Charles again dived down, forcing his wheels as close to the waves as he dared and flying in close formation with his shadow, alternating between masthead height and then flying so low that he was tempted to touch his tires on the water to break the monotony and see spray fly up. He was playing with dangerously small margins but believed these merely acted as stimulants to his flagging senses.

A second sign of life, this time a seagull, passed close to a wing tip, and then there was another visible in the distance. Charles wondered whether the presence of these birds indicated the nearness of land, but remembered he had heard of them following liners all the way across the ocean. How lucky they were to be able to land in the sea and have a snooze whenever they wished.

Suddenly a black speck caught his eye, and excitedly Charles realized that it was a small boat of the kind used for coastal fishing. Then he saw several others and decided to fly around for a closer look. There was no sign of life on the first, but on the second a man's head was framed in a porthole. No flags could be seen to indicate nationality. Sweeping into a turn, Charles came back low alongside, closed his throttle, and shouted at the top of his voice, "Which way is Ireland?" but on his return there was not the slightest response, so he gave up, not wanting to waste any more flying time.

In carrying out these maneuvers, Charles was horrified to discover that he had lost the feel of flying and could tell only by looking at his air-speed indicator whether he was danger-ously close to stalling speed. The pressure of the stick no longer imparted the message that it should.

At the turn of the twenty-eighth hour, he was flying at 100 feet, scanning the horizon ever more hopefully through breaks in the squalls. Only half-believing, he saw on the far horizon between two squalls a purple-blue band hardened in the haze. By this time, he was used to the trickery of mirages and was not going to be easily taken in. If this was Ireland, sixteen hours out from St. John's, he would be two and a half hours ahead of schedule for this 1,887-mile leg. Still, the wind, blowing at up to 60 m.p.h. from the west, could easily have done that to him, and this sudden hope brought back full wakefulness. Responding to the temptation to investigate, he turned sharply to the nearest point that he thought was land and, hardly able to believe his eyes, picked out a coast with rugged shores and rolling mountains beyond. Yes, it really was land! Here was a fjorded coast with barren islands (the Skelligs), and from 2,000 feet he could discern an outline that placed him without doubt at Valencia Island in Dingle Bay on Ireland's west coast, barely three miles from his intended landfall. What a relief and what a magnificent achievement! One would not think an error of three miles too bad on the twenty-mile crossing of the English Channel, but here after nearly 2,000 miles through all kinds of weather, Charles had hit Ireland almost exactly where he had wanted.

In acknowledging the wonders of white foam on black rocks, of curving hills, of little houses, and of welcoming, waving arms, Charles later wrote in *The Spirit of St. Louis*, "During my entire life I've accepted these gifts of God to man, and not known what was mine until this moment. It's like rain after drought; spring after a northern winter. I've been to eternity and back. I know how the dead would feel to live again."

Now it seemed so utterly easy—so long as the weather held —to go on to Paris and land in the dark in six hours' time. After concentrating on the charts and his onward route, Charles was amazed to look out and see nothing but ocean ahead until he realized that in his excitement he had turned the machine completely round. He soon put that right and delighted in flying low over the Irish farmland with its small houses and grazing sheep. Gone was the wish to sleep, and a new surge of vigor filled his being. All the strain of the ocean crossing had vanished, and now the weather was improving. From the corner of Ireland, he had just struck out across St. George's Channel when a change in engine note was followed by a dead cut. Charles immediately diagnosed the cause as being fuel starvation and quickly changed over to the center wing tank, giving a few vigorous jabs to the wobble pump, which brought the Whirlwind engine back to life with the loss of a few hundred feet.

In order to be sure of crossing England well before sunset, Charles pushed his cruising speed up to 110 m.p.h., for he still had plenty of fuel—although he knew he must have already broken the world's long-distance record—in fact, he estimated it enough for another thousand miles more than would be needed to reach Paris. He even thought of going on to Rome, but was discouraged by the possibility of running out of fuel over the mountains in darkness.

Three hours out from Valencia, he was relieved to find the cliffs of Cornwall with no fringe of fog and could see the amazingly small fields spread out like a map. He could not imagine the possibility of mechanized farming in such conditions. By the look of the sun, there was still about an hour's daylight. Beside him lay Plymouth, the port from which so many of his compatriots had originated, and he left England at Start Point, with eighty-five miles to go for the eastern corner of the Cap de la Hague and then the last little sea crossing to Deauville, which he passed over in the afterglow of sunset. This was the moment Charles chose for his first "meal," a single, very stale meat sandwich, which he described as tasting rather flat. "Bread and meat never touched my tongue like this before," he later wrote in *The Spirit of St. Louis*—and no wonder the other four sandwiches remained untouched.

From his present altitude, 2,000 feet, the Seine was easily picked out in the gathering darkness, and he climbed to 4,000 feet in order to be sure of seeing the glow of Paris. It started as a barely perceptible glimmer building up within half an hour to the full majesty of the French capital, and there for positive identification was the Eiffel Tower. Charles had been told that Le Bourget lay northeast of the city center but was not sure how far out and so headed that way, seeking vainly for a locator beacon. There was a black patch large enough for an airfield, but the lights around resembled factory buildings. After flying for five minutes beyond and seeing nothing that looked likely, he returned and spotted a concrete apron with planes on it.

As a precaution, he circled several times to lose altitude and made a dummy run. On slowing down the *Spirit of St. Louis*, how strange the controls felt. He realized how important it was to avoid stalling, but his movements seemed strangely uncoordinated. For the final run, he came in fast, aiming just short of some floodlights but overshooting them considerably, having to sideslip. Then, sensing that he was about to stall, in spite of his speed and the fact that there was really plenty of fuel left in the controls, he bounced once by the lights and then again as the *Spirit of St. Louis* was enveloped in darkness. How on earth he finished off without coming to any harm, exhausted as he was, on this, the first night-landing he had ever made in such a blind plane—and on a strange aerodrome (airfield)—was nothing short of a miracle. Then, on turning to taxi in, he encountered a crowd of Parisians running to welcome him.

Charles, after being virtually pulled out of his airplane by the throng, was rescued by someone with the brilliant notion of tearing off his flying helmet and planting it on the head of an American journalist, who became a decoy just long enough for Charles to be smuggled into a darkened hangar by two famous pilots, Delage and Detroyat. The smuggling operation was necessary because two companies of soldiers and the civil police had been powerless to restrain the mob, such was the enthusiasm of the French.

As always, Charles's main preoccupation on the ground was for the safety of his plane. He would not leave its vicinity until he was assured that a guard had been posted, though not before souvenir hunters had begun to wrench off fittings. At first, conversation in the hangar was difficult because neither

Lindbergh's *Spirit of St. Louis* at San Diego after completing all its tests

Working on the Wright Whirlwind 220-h.p. J-5 engine of his airplane before the Atlantic flight

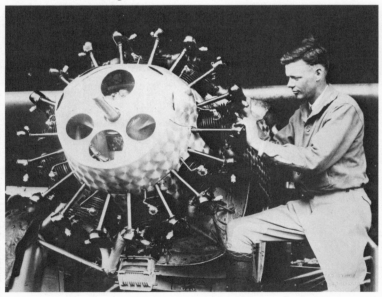

With "Keep out of the water" sign in New York, May, 1927
(Ryan Aeronautical Library)

◀

Pilot's view from the cockpit of the *Spirit of St. Louis*. The lever on the left is the tail-trimmer; the throttle and carburetor-heater controls are behind that and out of view. The lever on the dashboard is the mixture control. Overhead is the ordinary compass, and next to the altimeter is the dial for the earth-inductor compass. Note the complicated array of some of the fourteen fuel cocks to control the five tanks. Out of sight is the hand magneto, which the pilot had to crank—and crank and crank—in order to start the engine (Ryan Aeronautical Library)

The Skeldigs and Valencia Island as seen by Charles Lindbergh when he made landfall in Ireland on May 21, 1927 (Kelly Rogers)

▲

A Gallic salutation in Paris from M. Blériot, the first man to pilot an airplane across the English Channel

▼

▶   ▶   ▶

(Top left) Received by royalty in England. Lindbergh with the Prince of Wales and Lord Lonsdale *(left)* in the Royal Box at the Derby ball (Wide World Photos)

(Top right) The reception by President Coolidge on June 11, 1927, in front of the Washington Monument in Washington, D.C. (United Press International)

(Bottom) The procession up Broadway in New York City, amid a ticker-tape "snowstorm" (Wide World Photos)

of the French pilots spoke much English, but they were soon joined by Baron Willi Coppins, the Belgian ace and air attaché, who spoke English fluently. This eased the tension for Charles, who readily agreed to take an early opportunity to fly the *Spirit of St. Louis* to Brussels. He astonished Coppins by producing from his pocket a piece of paper with the name of a Paris hotel on it, and said, "Do you know this place, because I was told in New York that it was quite reasonable?" Charles also expressed concern that his passport bore no French visa, but the laughter that greeted his announcement of this news seemed to suggest that perhaps, in the circumstances, the omission might be overlooked. The four aviators were joined in the unlighted hangar by the military commandant, who insisted on driving them across the field to his office. After a long wait, the U.S. ambassador, Myron T. Herrick, managed to find them and invited Charles to stay at the embassy. In spite of lacking sleep for more than sixty hours, Charles would not leave the field without seeing the *Spirit of St. Louis*, although the French assured him that it was under armed guard in a locked hangar.

When he entered that locked hangar, Charles had a shock: the fuselage was full of gaping holes, and even a lubricator had been ripped off one of the engine's cylinder heads. In spite of appearances, Charles realized that the damage was superficial and could be repaired without too much difficulty. At this stage, the ambassador seemed to have become lost, so Charles was driven into the city with Detroyat and Commandant Weiss by Delage in a small, undistinguished-looking Renault, via a roundabout route in order to avoid the crowds blocking the normal ways to Le Bourget. By special request of his hosts, Charles's first stop was made at the Tomb of the Unknown Soldier in order to stand there silently for a few moments before going on to the embassy, where the ambassador caught up with them at three o'clock in the morning. By then,

Charles was glad to have been given a light supper. Herrick thereupon arranged a conference with the waiting newsmen, and at 4:15 A.M. Charles finally went to bed—just sixty-three hours since he had last slept.

When Charles awoke that afternoon, he began to learn what a worldwide sensation his terrific achievement had become. And for its part, the world, with France right in the forefront, applauded this tall, good-looking young man, whom his own countrymen had dubbed the "Flying Fool" but whose flight was the highlight of trans-Atlantic enterprise. He represented the All-American youth and the pioneering tradition that has marked the United States from its very beginning.

As soon as he had breakfasted, Charles appeared on the balcony of the embassy to be greeted by happy cheers from a crowd of French people. In a whirlwind tour during his week in Paris, he called on Mme. Nungesser, mother of the missing French flier, and encouraged her not to give up hope for her pilot son. He then visited President Gaston Doumergue, who pinned the insignia of the Legion of Honor on him. At the Aero Club de France he met Louis Blériot, who kissed him on both cheeks. There Charles made the first of his many public speeches. It was well received. Considering Charles's disjointed education, it was really amazing how well he expressed himself both orally and in writing. He praised Nungesser and Coli, saying they had attempted a much more difficult flight than his because they were headed against the prevailing wind, and he urged the French people not to give up hope.

One of the many functions Charles had to attend was the official reception by the City of Paris, when half a million people lined the streets to see him. More to his liking was the gesture of the Armée de l'Air in placing a Nieuport fighter at his disposal, and at Le Bourget he delighted the crowd with a polished display of stunt flying.

Charles spent a morning checking over the *Spirit of St. Louis* in the hangar and took off for Brussels at 1:00 P.M. on May 28. He was greeted at the airport by the Belgian prime minister and a well-controlled crowd, taken to a reception at the palace to meet King Albert, Queen Elizabeth, and Crown Prince Leopold, and as in France there were the presentations of medals and high honors.

The following day, May 29, Charles pressed on to London in the afternoon to be greeted by three welcoming biplanes, and then he was horrified to see that Croydon Airport, where he was to land, was almost covered by a swarm of human beings. Because of the mob, his first attempt to land was unsuccessful, and he just managed to get down on the second try, in spite of the presence of 1,300 policemen. Then his plane was immediately surrounded and he had to be rescued by officials of the Royal Aero Club, who dashed up in a car.

A dinner at the Savoy Hotel was given by the British press, and before the guest of honor was placed a plate bearing five sandwiches and a large jug of water. Calling for order, the chairman opened the evening by joking, "Captain Lindbergh will now partake of his customary meal."

On May 31, Charles had to fly the *Spirit of St. Louis* down to Gosport on the south coast, where the Royal Air Force was going to pack it for the journey home. Originally, President Coolidge had proposed sending a destroyer to fetch Charles, but to Charles's disappointment, this had been changed to the cruiser *Memphis*, and he would catch it at Cherbourg.

Charles was received by King George and Queen Mary at Buckingham Palace and invested with the Air Force Cross, which was the highest peacetime decoration of the R.A.F. It was sometimes said in jest that the Air Force Cross was given for flying in the face of the clock, but the Distinguished Flying Cross for flying in the face of the enemy, since the British D.F.C. could not be given in peacetime. When in private conversation with King George, Charles was surprised by being asked a personal question about the provision Charles had made for relieving himself during the flight. To this, Charles promptly replied that he had brought with him a well-corked aluminum flask, to serve as a urinal. The flask had not been needed until he was eighteen hours out of New York, and he had thrown it overboard before he reached Paris. This story was omitted from both *We: Pilot and Plane* and *The Spirit of St. Louis*, but it was told in Harold Nicolson's Diary.

Charles was received separately by the Prince of Wales, who asked him what he intended to do next. Charles promptly answered, "Keep on flying."

He also met Prime Minister Stanley Baldwin and was again taken to dinner at the Savoy, this time by the Royal Aero Club in conjunction with the Air League, presided over by the air minister, Lord Thomson, who in a welcoming speech said prophetically, "You may well find the perils of publicity greater than the perils of the Atlantic." Charles gave an excellent, completely unaffected description of his flight.

On June 2, Charles drove out to Kenley aerodrome, where the R.A.F. had placed a Hawker Woodcock fighter at his disposal for the trip to Paris, but he was grounded by fog and had to spend the night with the R.A.F. He got off soon after daybreak, only to be forced down by fog at Lympne on the coast, where he was able to take off again by following a radio-equipped Handley-Page airliner to Le Bourget. Next day, the French Armée de l'Air flew him in a Breguet XIX bomber with an escort of twenty planes to Cherbourg, where he joined the U.S.S. *Memphis*, which had picked up the *Spirit of St. Louis* at Portsmouth.

Five days later, Charles entered Chesapeake Bay on his

cruiser, accompanied by destroyers, blimps, and planes at the beginning of the greatest reception given to any man in the history of the United States. On the following day in Washington everything that could demonstrate national joy was used —church bells, factory whistles, formations of aircraft (including even the great airship *Los Angeles*)—and throngs milled everywhere in the hope of catching a glimpse of their hero as he drove in state through the streets with an escort of cavalry and bands to be received, with his mother, at the Washington Monument by President Coolidge, who, having already promoted Charles to colonel, bestowed upon him the Distinguished Flying Cross. Of course this was accompanied by a speech—a rather long one—but once again, Charles showed in his reply a simplicity and sincerity that endeared him to his audience.

In the evening a reception was given by the National Press Club in the Washington Auditorium, and, among other presentations, Charles received the Smithsonian Institution's Medal of Pioneers, an award hitherto given only to men such as Eiffel, Orville Wright, and Glen Curtiss.

Of the many messages from various cities and countries, one from the British Government read, "The British people regard Colonel Lindbergh with special admiration and affection not only for his great courage and resource, but also for his equally great modesty in success and generosity in giving their due to other aviators who have gone before."

In his speech Charles explained that he had really wanted to travel around Europe, only to be informed that "while it was not necessarily an order to come back home, there was a battleship waiting for me. The Ambassador said it wasn't an order, but advice!"

He went on to declare that he found Europe ahead of America in passenger airlines but behind her in airmail. He therefore thought America had to expand her passenger services, for, as a country, she had enormous advantages in the great distances and in not being hindered by the political obstruction of international frontiers. He finished by saying, "What we need now more than any other one thing is a series of airports in every city and town throughout the United States. Given these airports, in a very few years the nations of Europe would be looking toward our passenger lines as they now look at our mail routes"—a prophecy that soon became a reality because of the terrific impetus given to airline development by the flight of Charles Lindbergh.

After three days in Washington, Charles went to New York, borrowing a fighter from the army for this journey while the engine of the *Spirit of St. Louis* was being tuned. His nostalgic New York arrival consisted of landing at Mitchel Field, transferring to a Loening amphibian, which was to land in the harbor near Mayor James Walker's private launch, where he would be officially received by the people of New York. When Charles's seaplane came overhead, he was confronted with a fantastic array of boats of every size and description imaginable. The waters of the Hudson were so thickly covered that it seemed as if everything that could float had been thrown in! Never in New York's history had such a large number of boats been assembled: there must have been at least four hundred vessels crowding into the water below the Battery.

As soon as the Loening had landed, it was first met by a police launch, which took Charles to Mayor Walker's *Macom*, to the accompaniment of an earsplitting screech from all the sirens. This continued at such a pitch that during the ensuing voyage to the Battery, where fire hoses were cascading torrents of water into the air, conversation among the mayor's party, which included the press, was almost impossible, and to the din was added the noise of many planes circling overhead.

On shore at the Battery, the crowds were thicker than ever —the number was estimated at over four million. As the cavalcade drove up Broadway, a deluge of ticker tape, confetti, and any handy paper was streaming out of all the surrounding windows in such quantity that films taken of the event showed the scene just as though a snowstorm had started. At City Hall, Mayor Walker had to make another speech, and Charles in his reply said that his New York reception equaled those of Le Bourget, Brussels, London, and Washington rolled into one. Appropriately, and with due ceremony, he went on to lay a wreath at the Shaft of Eternal Light in Madison Square.

More functions and ceremonies followed for a whole week, and on June 15, Charles dined on the yacht of Rodman Wanamaker, went to the opera, attended a charity benefit show at a theater from which he escaped through a back door, and was driven to Mitchel Field. Still in his evening clothes, he borrowed a flying helmet and took off in an army fighter for Washington so that he could shuttle back to New York the next morning in his beloved *Spirit of St. Louis,* ready to face one more day of festivities, ending with the award of the check for $25,000 by Raymond Orteig at the Waldorf-Astoria Hotel.

On June 17, Charles set out from New York for the nine-hour flight to St. Louis and was joined by a formation of thirty army fighters as he passed over Dayton. Because of heavy mist, visibility was poor on the run in to Lambert Field, but Charles knew the area well, and he landed safely, to find a cordon of troops waiting to guard him and his plane. Here the reception by the crowds was as enthusiastic as ever—for hadn't Charles Lindbergh made the relatively obscure name of St. Louis known all over the world? And wasn't it in St. Louis that the nine daring and enterprising businessmen had been found to put up the money for Charles's venture? Fortunately, the hero was allowed a quiet evening with friends before the city parade next day, to be followed by a huge lunch and then a banquet in the evening and the all-too-familiar pattern of eulogies calling for one more speech by Charles.

Ever since he had reached Paris, Charles had been receiving, in addition to awards,* an endless cascade of mail—offers of money, jobs, high fees for appearances, marriage, and many simple messages of good will. An estimate put the number of letters at two million, and in addition to the letters, there were hundreds of thousands of telegrams. Charles could not answer all those messages but he did issue a statement of thanks, through the press, to all those who had written him, and explained that it was impossible for him to acknowledge every piece of mail.

What an intensely exciting and exhausting week it had been! If any final proof were needed of Charles's stamina on the ground, it could be found in the way he finished off his homecoming tour.

---

* Lindbergh's entire collection of gifts, medals, trophies, and gold keys to cities including London and Paris is listed in *The Spirit of St. Louis*.

CHAPTER III ✦ The Analysis

Why had this solo flight been such an astonishing success? Above all, Charles Lindbergh had demonstrated to the world the impact of the plane's range on transoceanic communications by flying from New York to Paris nonstop in 33 hours, 30 minutes, 29.8 seconds (F.A.I. official time) at an average speed of 107.9 m.p.h. He had thereby broken the world's long-distance record, which, when he took off, stood at 3,353 statute miles, from Paris to Jask in the Persian Gulf, set by André Codos and Marcel Rignot. Actually, while Lindbergh was in flight, this record had again been broken by Roderick Carr and Leslie Gillman, who covered 3,420 miles until forced down in the same gulf, near Bandar Abbas, just six hours before Lindbergh reached Paris with his still better distance of 3,614 miles. As a footnote to this spate of broken records, Chamberlain and Levine flew the Bellanca (which Lindbergh had wanted to buy) nonstop from New York to Eisleben, 120 miles short of Berlin, two weeks later, a distance of 3,910 miles, but the effect of this two-man flight was quite secondary to that of the Lindbergh flight, despite its greater length.

In fact, the breaking of the world's long-distance record, although a fine technical achievement, was the lesser part of Charles's accomplishment. Its true significance was that it brought home the message of aviation in terms challenging and dramatic to the ordinary citizen, who had hitherto regarded airplanes as rather dangerous contraptions.

C. R. Smith, president of American Airlines, stated: "Before Lindbergh there was spasmodic interest in the flying machine, and there was nearly no investor interested in wanting to put his money into so financially hazardous an undertaking. Lindbergh's flight created an atmosphere in which people wanted to invest a lot of money in aviation."

Charles saw himself not so much a pioneer as a torch-bearer, bringing the message of aviation to the people of America. In fact, he did far more than that, for his epoch-making flight acted as a catalyst on world opinion and inspired a great surge of optimism in favor of developing civil aircraft and civil airlines everywhere, not just in the United States.

In my last letter to Charles, in February, 1974, I remarked that his Paris flight, involving fifty-seven and one-half hours without sleep, would always stand out as the high-water mark of human endurance in solo flying. He replied with his characteristic and entirely genuine modesty: "I am afraid I do disagree with you about the importance of solo flying. I think this came out in the correspondence we had in regard to that excellent book you wrote, *Challenge to the Poles.* As I recall, you felt that the primary importance of my flight from New York to Paris in 1927 lay in the fact that I flew solo whereas I feel that the primary importance (at least in describing it) lay in the fact that it was the first nonstop airplane flight between the continents of North America and Europe. I flew alone because I felt it was more practical, simpler and less complicated and expensive. (See *The Spirit of St. Louis.*)" Thus, he brushed aside completely the elements of courage and determination that were his alone, especially in going on after reaching the safety of Ireland to land in the dark on an unknown Paris aerodrome.

The performance of striking Ireland within three miles of his intended landfall was unprecedented.* Yet, on Charles's own admission, there had been periods when he had made many uncontrolled course changes, owing to weather conditions or fatigue, and when he had neglected his navigation to an alarming extent. The act of diving low over a fishing boat to shout, "Which way is Ireland?" was proof that, so far as facts and figures were concerned at that time, Lindbergh was uncertain about his navigation. Was it pure luck that he succeeded to such an exceptional degree or did the latent homing instinct of man come to his aid during the flight at moments of highest tension and greatest need?

This little-recognized power is something I have long suspected from my own flying experiences, but for which until recently I have not seen sufficiently strong evidence to justify making a public claim. For instance, the best landfall I have ever made was in 1933 on reaching Iceland after flying 360 miles from the Faeroes in five and a half hours in my Gypsy Moth seaplane *Rouge et Noir*. It was Bank Holiday, so no weather forecast was available, and as I later discovered, my course ran through the centers of two deep depressions signaled by pouring rain, low cloud, and heavy seas, during which, due to sticking valves, my engine began to run intermittently on three cylinders. I did not really expect to reach land before it failed altogether, my navigation was forgotten, and I was absolutely scared stiff. Yet, somehow I hit Iceland

* Alcock and Whitten Brown were about forty miles from Galway, their aiming point, when they hit Ireland at Clifden.

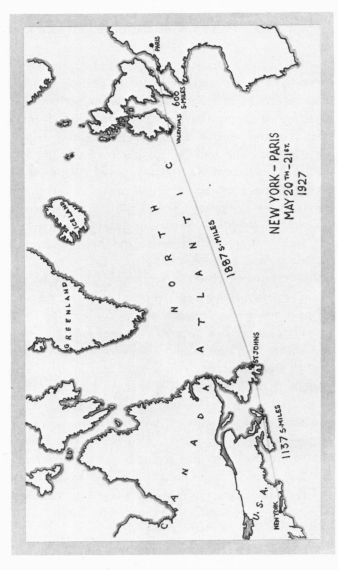

The route flown by Charles Lindbergh on May 20-21, 1927, between Roosevelt Field, Long Island, and Le Bourget, Paris (Sheila Innes)

within half a mile of my aiming point—a very minor achievement compared to Charles's, but the elements of high tension and great need were similar. Like him I had the sensation of going across the bridge and somehow miraculously coming back again.

Another time, on the way down the Hudson Bay, while over complete cloud cover, in my Fox Moth seaplane *Robert Bruce*, I was running low on fuel and wanted to land. Suddenly, there was a small break in the cloud, and I spotted a tiny church, marking the settlement of Fort George, the point at which my fuel would run out. When I had landed on the river, I was told by the station manager that ten minutes earlier, I would never have found the settlement, which, until the few minutes before I landed, had been entirely shrouded by mist and cloud.

I had always accepted Francis Chichester's solo Tasman flight in a Gypsy Moth seaplane when he successively hit two tiny landmarks, Lord Howe and Norfolk Islands, as the greatest feat of solo navigation. Had he missed either island, he was certain to have been drowned, and I believed that it was entirely due to superb astro-navigation, despite the fact that all the experts, including Charles Lindbergh,* said this could not be done. How could anyone fly a plane on an absolutely steady course and take accurate sights of the sun at the same time? Having known Francis Chichester for many years, I believed that he had achieved this seemingly impossible feat of taking sights. I am sure he himself thought that this alone was how he had found the two small targets. But in contradistinction to this very high degree of achieved accuracy, when he went on from Norfolk Island with all the pressure and ten-

* When lecturing R.A.F. cadets at Cranwell in 1936, Charles remarked, "Some people say that they can read a bubble sextant when flying solo, but I can't."

sion of aiming at a solitary island having been removed, he was actually eighty miles out in his final landfall on the mainland of Australia.

Within the last couple of years I have seen evidence that has led me to reassess the meanings of navigational results in flights like the above ones of Charles, myself, and Francis Chichester. It really seems that in our subconscious minds some, especially under conditions of strain and emotion, do possess a remarkably strong sense of direction toward unseen things or people in which we are vitally interested—the greater the need, the greater the sensitivity. (Someone I know very well who \\as the aptitude for water-divining, using a brazed Tee-rod of welding wire, has found that her rod will also point toward people when she is thinking of them.) I am convinced that certain people have hidden extrasensory abilities that are ready and waiting to serve their needs. And I submit that it was just the strength of this, and not navigation in the ordinary sense of the word, that led Charles to within three miles of his aiming point on Ireland. He himself, without attempting to name the cause of his success, wrote in *The Spirit of St. Louis* that "luck seems far too trivial a word" for it.

Although in planning his Paris flight Charles had thought about so many problems in great detail, it must be remarked in retrospect that there were several areas that, if not actually overlooked, did receive less attention than the rest. Briefly, these were:

1. Practice in overwater flying—Charles had never flown across any sea before May 20, 1927;
2. Practice in night-landing the *Spirit of St. Louis*—the lack of forward vision in the Ryan introduced a special problem in its handling;
3. An assessment of the value of the periscope—in the first

hour Charles remarked in his log that the periscope would enable him to sit in the center of the cockpit and avoid fatigue, but some pages further on he remarked, "watching the periscope mirror is an added strain";

4. Flight-planning based on a great-circle track from New York to Paris, which was plotted in March but made irrelevant with the diversion to St. John's, ninety miles south of the track he had drawn;

5. His inclination to fly extremely low even when not forced to do so by the weather—based on a hypothesis about performance benefit from the boundary layer;

6. His estimate of the potential extra range of the *Spirit of St. Louis* when it landed at Le Bourget with eighty-five gallons left, apparently derived from theoretical rather than practical considerations.

Flying over water: To those who live in the maritime countries of Europe, it seems almost impossible to imagine that a pilot could have amassed 2,000 flying hours without having flown out of sight of land other than when obscured by cloud. But such was the case with Charles's flying over the huge land mass of North America, which makes it all the more remarkable that he never sought to practice his navigation or simply see what it felt like when flying over water—he could easily have made a 250-mile sea crossing to the island of Guadalupe, to the south-southwest of San Diego, during his flight trials. He thus went in "off the deep end" on May 20, as he winged his way north past Cape Cod, intending to employ a drift sight he had never tried before (and in the end elected not to use), but actually deciding to estimate the strength and direction of the wind by looking at the waves. Nevertheless, at the first attempt he achieved very reasonably satisfactory results by making landfall on Nova Scotia within six miles of his aim and, after that, he never looked back. Personally, I have tried both the simple method of drift-reading such as Charles practiced, and the employment of a drift sight built into the floor of the cockpit. Although the latter was rather convenient for looking through as one held a steady course, I doubt that it was much more accurate in practice. Fortunately, Charles's untried navigation methods did work out all right, and so the fact that he had not practiced them did not matter at all.

Night-landings: The absence of any practice night-landings in the *Spirit of St. Louis* seemed all the stranger because Charles knew so much about night-flying and night-landing under the very worst conditions, which might have made him approach the problems of landing the Ryan at night with respect if not reverence. On paper this was going to be much more difficult than any landing Charles had ever done before: the aircraft more "blind" than any other; the airfield strange and lighted differently from the ones at home; the pilot at the end of thirty-three and a half hours, when fatigue problems such as double vision might well rear their ugly heads. In short, Charles had almost everything possible against him at Le Bourget, but he proceeded to land without killing himself or even grazing his plane, so once again the lack of practice did not matter at all.

The periscope: The periscope was really the brain child of one of the mechanics at Ryans. In *The Spirit of St. Louis*, Charles describes it as "a home-made device, built by one of the workmen in the factory at San Diego." It consisted of two flat mirrors set at a proper angle in a rectangular tube that could be extended out of the port side by the pilot on pushing a knob that slid across the panel. Charles remarked that there was no increase in air speed when he retracted this instrument. The field of vision was not large but gave enough view of the country immediately ahead to enable the pilot to see a hill, radio mast, or any other such obstruction in his path. But Charles stated categorically that the periscope was useless during taxiing, takeoff, and landing, so its value was distinctly limited. He had not had time to try it out properly during test flights, and it was particularly disappointing that it was of no help during takeoff and landing, when keeping the plane straight was so important. In flight Charles found the periscope fatiguing to watch, and he could not have gotten any use out of it during the latter part of his journey.

Flight-planning: The flight-planning carried out in San Diego was of a sound and simple nature. The plan was based on a great-circle course between Roosevelt Field and Le Bourget and was divided into hundred-mile stages, each of which was marked with a course that took into account local magnetic variation. At that time, Charles was very worried that one of the other contestants, such as Fonck, Byrd, or Levine, might succeed in making the Paris flight first. Charles therefore armed himself with a second set of charts, of the Pacific, and schemed out an alternate route to Hawaii, so that he could fly west, and perhaps all the way round the world, instead of east—just in case the Raymond Orteig Prize had been won before he could start.

He had to teach himself from the instructions he found printed on the charts how to lay out a great-circle course. Charles had never done anything like this before, so he was at first careful not to ask anyone too many questions in case he might appear to be unqualified for the Atlantic flight. All the same, he felt it was so supremely important to have all his courses and angles 100 percent right that he would have liked to ask an expert to check them for him. Instead, he went to the San Diego Public Library, intent on laying out a second route by trigonometry with the aid of navigation textbooks.

But first he had to teach himself the necessary mathematical procedures, which took several days, and then start drawing lines. Only then was he satisfied: on plotting each stage of a hundred miles, step by step, the new lines matched the previous ones so closely that after several more days, when he had reached a point 1,200 miles east of Newfoundland, Charles realized that no more checking was necessary.

At that stage it did not seem to have occurred to Charles that it might have been worth making a deviation at the cost of a very few miles—perhaps ten or twelve—in order to pass over St. John's as a safety measure in having the time of his departure from the American continent witnessed from the ground. Probably the reason for this was that the need to save fuel and obtain the maximum range from the *Spirit of St. Louis* was uppermost in his mind and, in this context, a "deviation" of any size was to be avoided.

On taking off from Roosevelt Field, Charles had every intention of hugging the great-circle course every inch of the way to Paris so far as weather and navigation would allow. What actually happened was that crosswinds and storms over Nova Scotia had carried the plane so far east that at the beginning of the ninth hour he would have had to change course 15° westward in order to strike his great-circle track at the point where he was to cross the south coast of Newfoundland. Clouds over the mountains were an incentive not to deviate toward the west, and so purely on the basis of the situation as it had developed over Nova Scotia, Charles decided to hold his course east of the great circle, which would bring him over St. John's.

This was an eminently satisfactory arrangement, for it ensured that all the anxious backers in St. Louis, the ground staffs at Ryans and at Roosevelt Field, and above all his mother would be relieved to know at least that he had safely

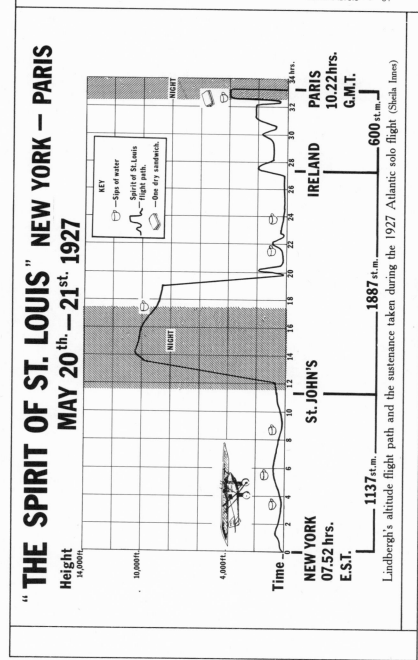

Lindbergh's altitude flight path and the sustenance taken during the 1927 Atlantic solo flight (Sheila Innes)

completed the first leg of the journey. The only slightly unto-ward feature was that Charles now knew he was ninety miles south of his great circle as plotted, and this was a recurring source of worry for many hours of his trans-Atlantic flight. It could have been eliminated in the preliminaries by drawing one great-circle track from Roosevelt Field to St. John's, then a further one on to Le Bourget.

Low-flying: Charles's tendency to fly extremely low when-ever the weather would let him seemed all the more surprising because he was expecting, and did actually experience most of the time, a tail wind. In general, if the wind is ahead, it pays to fly low because the wind strength naturally increases with altitude, but on the other hand, a tail wind gives more help with increasing height. Yet he often cruised below 100 feet—indeed, at 50, 20, or even 5 feet, about which he wrote in *The Spirit of St. Louis* of "being tempted to touch my tires on the water to break the monotony and see spray fly up." I greatly regret that during Charles's lifetime I never took the opportunity to question him about why he flew so exhaustingly low, because it must have called for much more concentration at a time when he was desperately oppressed by the desire to sleep. It was not until I had studied his story in greater de-tail that I was struck by the high proportion of flight time that Charles spent very close to the sea.

The only clue to his thoughts on this technique appeared in *We: Pilot and Plane,* when he wrote:

> There is a cushion of air close to the ground or water through which a plane flies with less effort than when at a higher altitude, and for hours at a time I took advantage of this factor.
>
> Also, it was less difficult to determine the wind drift near the water. During the entire flight the wind was strong enough to produce white caps on the waves.

Much serious investigation into the performance benefit of flying in the boundary layer had already taken place by the time of Charles's Paris flight, notably by his countryman Dr. E. P. Warner (later to become "father" of the International Civil Aviation Organization). Warner found that biplanes and low-wing monoplanes had a geometrical advantage not shared by high-wing ones such as the *Spirit of St. Louis*, whose wing was eight feet above the bottom of the tires. In his book *Airplane Design*, Dr. Warner wrote that if the wing could have been kept near enough to the surface (either water or earth) "the freedom of the escape of air from under the trailing edge being interfered with, the velocity of flow over the lower surface is reduced, and the pressure on that surface is increased."

Thus, with a high-wing monoplane, unlike a low-wing one or a biplane, ground effect could never have an important influence on maximum lift. For the same reason, induced drag could never be as favorable under low-flying conditions with a high-wing monoplane as with biplanes or low-wing monoplanes, where gains in maximum speed of the order of 1 to 3 percent have been recorded by flying as close as possible to the surface of level ground or smooth water in a calm atmosphere.

Another influence on performance is the power of the engine, which, in the case of a naturally aspirated engine—such as the Whirlwind was—would fall with the reduction of atmospheric pressure to .971 of the ground value at 1,000 feet, and progressively thereafter. However, because we are concerned with cruising as opposed to maximum speed, this 2.9 h.p. per 100 h.p. of the engine's rating can be recovered by opening the throttle slightly, which means that there would be no significant gain in cruising very low on this account.

One is therefore bound to deduce that only if Charles had been flying the *Spirit of St. Louis* under conditions of head wind might he have gained any benefit by cruising very low, and then not for the reason of improved performance of the plane but of reduced strength of the wind close to the surface. In fact, such was *not* the condition of the flight to Paris; he benefited from a tail wind across the Atlantic of a strength ranging up to at least 60 m.p.h. at times.

Given a clear sky, the limiting factor of how high Charles could reasonably have flown was that he should not have risked exposure to upper wind from a direction appreciably different from that on the surface, where he was interpreting its sense and strength by his observations. He could certainly have stayed up at 3,000 or 4,000 feet much of the time when he was skittering along at 100 or 50 feet, and this not only would have benefited his ground speed, but also would have reduced fatigue caused by the knife-edge concentration necessary to fly his very unstable plane and his unceasing battle to keep himself awake.

It must have been the story that other pilots had told him which impressed Charles with the need to fly so extremely low, in the belief that he was thereby reaping a useful performance benefit from "boundary-layer effect." This belief was certainly prevalent a few years ago—I suffered from it myself—and it may have been due, in part at least, to the sensation, when one is engrossed in the joys of hedge-hopping, that things seem to be going past the window quite noticeably faster than if one were flying a little bit higher.

Clearly, if Charles had flown higher whenever he could, he would have made Paris in even better time and increased the safety margin during the many moments when he was on the brink of succumbing to sleep. Equally clearly, nothing said with hindsight about how he might have conducted his flight can in the least alter the fact that he succeeded so handsomely in flying the way he did.

Potential range: Charles's speed on the basis of the distance he had *actually* flown when he arrived in Paris must have been higher than the official 107.9 m.p.h. average for the great-circle distance from New York, because of the extra mileage involved by his course variations. En route from St. John's to Valencia, Charles's weather diversions, periods of magnetic instability, and the variability of his course-keeping when he was so tired in a very unstable plane were superimposed on the fact that for many hours he was flying out of sight of the surface. He was then quite unable to make any adjustments to his course on account of crosswinds or know where he was being carried in the upper atmosphere. Neither Charles nor anybody else could ever know how many extra miles he actually flew over the Atlantic, but it could easily have been 10 percent, that is, 189 miles, or even more. In addition, he was over Paris for at least a quarter of an hour before he landed at Le Bourget due to difficulty in locating the strange field and the need for a dummy run before he landed. Thus, if one credits him with his minimum likely extra mileage and deducts the time he spent over Paris from his overall flight time, he would have flown 3,803 miles in 33 hours, 15 minutes at an average speed of 114.4 m.p.h. This theory merely serves to underscore what a fantastic performance Charles's was for a single man in a plane of only 220 hp.

The potential ability of the *Spirit of St. Louis* to go on flying beyond Paris deserves to be examined carefully, in order to decide what the true maximum range of the little plane would have been. Of the 450 gallons on board at the start, eighty-five were found to be still there when the French mechanics drained the *Spirit of St. Louis*'s tanks. This was after covering the point-to-point mileage of 3,614 miles, and Charles estimated that by flying on at the most economical cruising speed of about 70 m.p.h. (with the greatly reduced load) he could have continued for 1,040 miles. However, it presupposes test conditions rather than those of a cross-country night-flight, when the en-route weather and topography often demand unforeseen speed and power changes detrimental to fuel consumption.

Charles had intended, when he made up his original plan, to cruise initially at 95 m.p.h., gradually reducing this to 75 m.p.h. as the fuel load was lightened, but in fact he started by cruising at between 102 and 107 m.p.h., as indicated by his hourly log, then reduced slowly to 92 m.p.h.; and when he had climbed to 9,300 feet at the start of the fourteenth hour out of New York, he cruised at between 85 and 90 m.p.h., which was appreciably more in terms of true air speed because of the lower density at high altitude. Then, on passing Ireland, he opened up to 110 m.p.h. in order to get as far as possible before darkness. All this proves how difficult it is in practice to adhere to a preplanned regime of economical air speed because there are so many practical factors, especially weather, that militate against it.

It therefore seems to me, though perhaps Charles would not have agreed, that in a case such as this, the potential extension of the range should be calculated as a fraction of the achieved range. In other words, if one bases one's estimate on the above revised figure of 3,803 miles during which 365 gallons were consumed and eighty-five unused, the air miles per gallon would be 10.419, and mileage on eighty-five gallons, 886. This seems fair because although with lightened load, the *Spirit of St. Louis* would require less engine power to cruise at a given speed, it is improbable that even if the tail wind persisted across Europe, it would have been nearly as strong as it had been over the open Atlantic. The overall potential of 3,803 plus 886 miles (4,689 miles) to dry tanks was still a remarkably fine achievement for a plane originally estimated to have a range of only 4,040 miles (the figure before they discovered that the fuel tank held twenty-five gallons more than their estimate).

It was Charles's unshakable belief that the importance of his New York–Paris flight lay in its being the first nonstop one between the continents of North America and Europe. Only history will decide whether his fantastic achievement was more remarkable on this account or because, as I and others believe, his feat of skill, courage, and stamina constituted the most remarkable solo flight in the history of man.

Chapter IV ✦ The Hero

Even before the high pressure of all the homecoming celebrations had subsided, Charles was planning his next step in order to take advantage of the terrific impact his New York–Paris solo epic had made. He wanted to convey the message of aviation to all the people of America. He wished to emphasize the good the airplane could do for the public, by providing rapid transportation for passengers, goods, and mail.

A pressing invitation came from Mr. William Mackenzie-King, prime minister of Canada, for Charles to visit Ottawa almost as soon as he had returned, and Charles was glad to respond by promising a flight with the *Spirit of St. Louis*. The visit would be regarded by all as a good-will gesture between the two countries.

Charles collected the *Spirit of St. Louis* from Washington and flew, via Roosevelt Field, first to Mitchel Field on June 17, and then on the next day to Lambert Field, St. Louis, where he remained until the end of the month. On July 1, he journeyed to Selfridge Field at Mount Clemens, Michigan, where he allowed his old commanding officer, Major Thomas Lanphier, to take his plane up on a ten-minute local flight. This was a rare distinction because up until then no one other than Charles had ever piloted the *Spirit of St. Louis*. Next day, he flew direct to Ottawa for his brief but diplomatic visit to Canada's prime minister, returning on July 4 to Teterboro, New Jersey.

In the next two weeks, Charles worked out a tremendous tour of the United States, on which he would land the *Spirit of St. Louis* in every state of the Union. The flight was organized under the sponsorship of Harry F. Guggenheim, president of the Daniel Guggenheim Fund for the Promotion of Aeronautics, and it included sixty-eight overnight stops and an elapsed time of three months, beginning on July 20. In addition to Charles and his plane, one publicity man was sent ahead by train, and a support aircraft, furnished by the Commerce Department, flew half an hour in front of the *Spirit of St. Louis*, carrying a Commerce Department representative, an engine mechanic, and a few spare parts.

A glance at the map shows what a comprehensive tour this was. It was extremely hard work for Charles because, besides flying almost every day and having the constant worry of someone's being sliced by his propeller whenever the mobs surged forward to greet him, he was lionized, had his hand shaken, was asked for his autograph, was banqueted, and had to make speeches wherever he went.

Although Charles landed in so many locations, there were also cities where, for one reason or another, he could not go down. For the people in those places he had devised a special procedure with a prepared message, enclosed in a canvas bag with long orange streamers. This bag he would drop on an open space near the city center. The message contained in the bag read as follows:

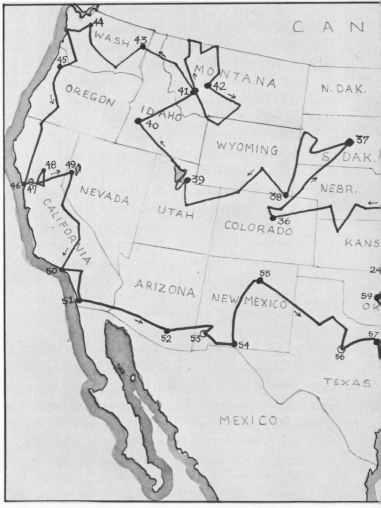

Route map of Lindbergh's second great flight, the 22,350-mile tour of the United States in the *Spirit of St. Louis*, which involved 260 flying hours between July 20 and October 23, 1927, based on the original map of the *National Geographic Magazine* (Sheila Innes)

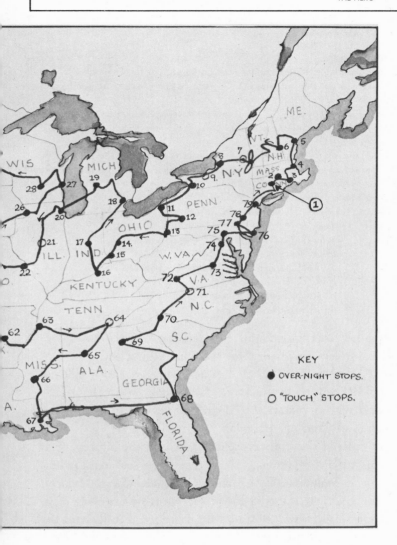

KEY

● OVER-NIGHT STOPS.

○ "TOUCH" STOPS.

Aboard *Spirit of St. Louis* on Tour.

Greetings:

Because of the limited time and the extensive itinerary of the Tour of the United States now in progress to encourage popular interest in aeronautics, it is impossible for the *Spirit of St. Louis* to land in your city.

This message from the air, however, is sent you to express our sincere appreciation of your interest in the Tour and in the promotions and extensions of commercial aeronautics in the United States.

We feel that we will be amply repaid for all our efforts if each and every citizen in the United States cherishes an interest in flying and gives his earnest support to the Air Mail Service and the establishment of airports and similar facilities. The concerted efforts of the citizens of the United States in this direction will result in America's taking its rightful place within a very short time, as the world leader in commercial flying.

[Signed]   *Charles A. Lindbergh*

Harry F. Guggenheim, President

Daniel Guggenheim Fund for the Promotion of Aeronautics

William P. McCracken Jr.

Assistant Secretary for Aeronautics

Department of Commerce

Weather was varied and included fog, cloud, and snow. This is not very surprising, for the tour did not end until October 23 and had a total of 260 hours logged and a mileage of 22,350 credited to the *Spirit of St. Louis*, all without mishap and with a remarkable degree of regularity due to the soundness of Charles's planning.

The idea of using his presence to help in the improvement of international relationships had not been lost on Dwight Morrow, Ambassador to Mexico. Since U.S.–Mexican friendship was at rather a low ebb, Morrow engineered an invitation from President Calles for Lindbergh to fly into the Mexican capital and, when the nature of the mission had been explained, Charles was very glad both of the opportunity to do a useful job for his country and to visit a land he had never seen before.

Accordingly, on December 13 Charles took off from Bolling Field in Washington, D.C. at 12:45 P.M. intent on making a nonstop flight to Mexico City, some 2,000 miles away. Unlike the Paris flight, when he was eastbound and actually shortening the time of darkness for himself by flying into the rising sun, he was now heading southwest, thereby having to contend with a much longer period of night. To add to his navigational difficulties, he found that the only maps of Mexico he could get in New York were little better than those in school atlases and were really inadequate for flying.

In his brief note on this flight in *The Spirit of St. Louis*, Charles wrote, "Flew via Texas coast of Gulf of Mexico. Lost position flying over fog between Tampico and Valley of Mexico. Climbed after fog cleared, and located approximate position from the direction of watersheds. Located exact position from sign on hotel wall at Toluca." He certainly showed an inventive turn of mind in making use of landmarks such as watersheds and hotel signs, neither of which had until then been given any space in the standard works of aerial navigation. He also tried reading the names of railway stations, but gave it up when he found they all seemed to be called Caballeros. As a result of these difficulties, Charles was some three hours late on estimate in reaching the Mexico City airport of Valbuena. The ambassador and reception committee were very relieved when the *Spirit of St. Louis* eventually touched down on the runway, which is there over 8,000 feet above sea level.

Naturally, Charles was invited to stay at the embassy, where he met the Morrow family: the ambassador and his wife, Elizabeth; three daughters, Elisabeth, Anne, and Constance; and a son, Dwight. As it was just before Christmas, the young people looked forward to a cozy family party and rather resented the intrusion of a public hero into their midst. The picture of Charles they had conjured up was not tremen-

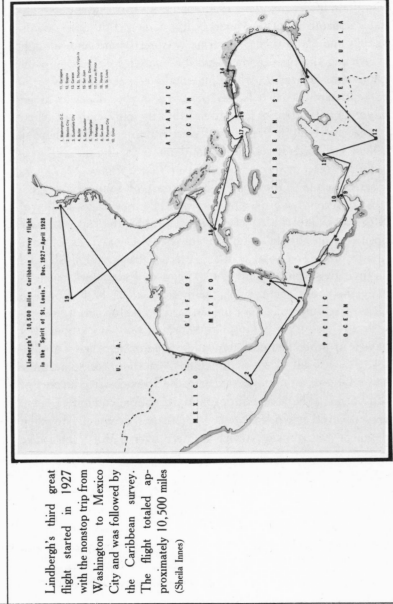

Lindbergh's 10,500 miles Caribbean survey flight
in the "Spirit of St. Louis." Dec. 1927—April 1928

1. Washington D.C.
2. Mexico City
3. Guatemala City
4. Belize
5. San Salvador
6. Tegucigalpa
7. Managua
8. San José
9. San José
10. Colon

11. Cartagena
12. Bogota
13. Caracas
14. St. Thomas, Virgin Is
15. San Juan
16. Santo Domingo
17. Port au Prince
18. Havana
19. St. Louis

Lindbergh's third great flight started in 1927 with the nonstop trip from Washington to Mexico City and was followed by the Caribbean survey. The flight totaled approximately 10,500 miles (Sheila Innes) dously attractive: good-looking, of course—they had seen that much from newspaper photographs—but a foreigner to the rather high-brow and intellectual standard of their diplomatic world. They just did not expect him to fit in. Anne stated in her book *Bring Me a Unicorn*, "I certainly was *not* going to worship 'Lindy' (that odious name, anyway)." But little did she know!

When Anne was introduced to Charles, after her elder sister, she remarked, ". . . a tall, slim boy in evening dress—so much slimmer, so much taller, so much more poised than I expected. A very refined face not at all like those grinning 'Lindy' pictures—a firm mouth, clear, straight blue eyes, fair hair and nice color. . . . He did not smile—just bowed and shook hands." Thus were the seeds sown.

After the festivities, from December 28 until February 13, 1928, Charles made a good-will tour, on the invitation of the countries visited: Guatemala, Honduras, Nicaragua, Costa Rica, Panama, Colombia, Venezuela, and then north to the Virgin Islands, Puerto Rico, Dominica, Haiti, and Cuba. From Cuba, he made a fifteen-and-a-half-hour direct flight to St. Louis. During this flight, Charles had considerable trouble with both compasses over the night-blackened Florida Strait, where all the stars were obscured by heavy haze. This 9,000-mile tour was carried out without mishap, however, and constituted the very last long-distance flight of the *Spirit of St. Louis* because, at the end of the month, Charles flew to Bolling Field so that the plane could be transported to the final resting-place of honor: the Smithsonian Institution. The *Spirit of St. Louis* would be a "bed-mate" to the Wright brothers' original biplane, in which Orville Wright made the world's first authenticated power-driven flight, on December 17, 1903.

Charles was a very private person, with something of a hermit streak inherited from his mother, and would have liked to return to a life of privacy. This was impossible, however, because he was very much in demand all over the states, and it was necessary for him to respond to those demands if he were to spread the message of civil aviation. On joining Transcontinental Air Transport (T.A.T., the forerunner of T.W.A.) as chairman of its technical committee, Charles found himself more and more a target of publicity. Whenever possible he slipped off to Mexico City, on one pretext or another; but commitments at home were considerable, and in the summer he led a U.S. Army Air Corps aerobatic team at the Los Angeles Air Races.

A year later—on February 12, 1929, to be precise—the Morrows proudly announced the engagement of their daughter Anne to Charles Lindbergh. (Anne said Charles used to visit her privately at the Morrows' Englewood, New Jersey, house, called Next Day Hill, and the proposal came quite suddenly.) After the engagement was announced, Charles was a frequent visitor to Mexico, where he'd take Anne flying. On one occasion, he flew her off for a picnic in a borrowed Stinson. When they became airborne after lunch, one of the wheels fell off. Because no seat belts were in the plane, Charles surrounded Anne with seat cushions and told her to hang on to the seat bottom before the inevitable crash landing, which turned them upside down. Anne was unhurt, but Charles dislocated his right shoulder, just as he had done on his second emergency parachute drop.

The wedding took place in considerable secrecy at the Morrows' Englewood house on May 27, 1929. The guests were confined to members of the two families, including Charles's mother (who had overcome her initial doubts about the engagement because the Morrows came from the East: that was considered by Midwesterners to be "snobbish" in those days). Anne wore a dress made by the local dress-maker, an old veil, and her bridal bouquet had been gathered in the garden by her sister Elisabeth. The service was given by the head of a nearby theological seminary. Charles's suspicion of the press and their wiles for getting photographs was such that not a single photographer was allowed and no guest used a camera. In 1970, writing in his *Wartime Journals*, Charles looked back on his marriage as "the wisest thing I ever did." The couple spent their honeymoon in a thirty-eight-foot cabin motor launch, hoping thereby to achieve seclusion. In spite of their wearing rough clothes and heavily tinted glasses as disguise, Charles and Anne were discovered by the press, which even resorted to the use of planes and motorboats in order to track them down, mindless of the privacy they sought.

Fortunately, at this point, Charles began his association with Juan Trippe, who had founded Pan American Airways, originally in Alaska where, as Trippe told me, the only transportation had hitherto been provided by dog sleds, which were unbelievably slow over the rough countryside. Thus, it is no exaggeration to say that dog sleds were the inspiration for the foundation of the great worldwide organization of the modern Pan American system. Charles also maintained his relationship with T.A.T. There were a number of proving flights to be made for both these fledgling airlines—Pan American mostly in Sikorsky amphibians to Latin America, and T.A.T. in Ford Tri-motors domestically—and this activity was very much to the liking of Charles and Anne.

At this time, Charles's thoughts were turning to the likely long-term trend of aviation development, and he believed that a way of harnessing rockets would have to be found as the only possible key to space travel. He therefore made a visit to the Du Pont Company, the vast chemical concern; he thought a company such as this would, more likely than anyone else, be able to understand the problems involved in building a very large, powerful rocket capable of breaking out into space. Du Pont, however, visualized very little prospect of being able to incorporate rocket fuels in an aviation vehicle on account of the terrific weight of combustible needed and because of the heavy lining of firebrick demanded by the combustion chamber. They could see no prospect in 1929 of rockets being developed for space travel.

After this discouraging interview, Charles was very interested to read in The *New York Times* an article about the work of the scientist Robert H. Goddard, who had begun experiments with a rocket motor in Massachusetts. He immediately sought out Goddard at Clark University and found that his ideas for multi-stage rocket development completely supported Charles's own vision of the future. Obviously, there was a tremendous amount of experimental ground to be covered, and that would require more funds than were available by way of Smithsonian grants. Charles therefore went to see Harry Guggenheim, whom he had met before his flight to Paris and who had supported his 22,000-mile propaganda flight around the states and had become a patron of aeronautical research. Daniel Guggenheim, the father of Harry, came to the rescue with a grant of $100,000 from the Guggenheim Fund for the Promotion of Aeronautics, to be spread over four years. The grant was an absolute boon at such a critical stage in Goddard's work.

For his personal use, Charles ordered a long-range two-seater touring monoplane from the Lockheed Company in Burbank, California. In America it was one of the first planes of its type to have an enclosed cockpit, which added much to the crew's comfort and improved performance. Like most airplanes, it was not delivered on time, so Charles and Anne had to wait in San Diego for nearly three months. During the wait,

Charles did extensive soaring along the Pacific cliffs near Soledad Mountain at the invitation of Hawley Bowlus, the glider designer, and Anne became the first woman in America to qualify for her glider's license.

On obtaining delivery at Easter of the new sleek and efficient Lockheed, the Lindberghs flew it across the continent to New York via St. Louis in 14 hours, 45 minutes, thereby breaking the record by three hours. Anne, trained by the famous navigator Harold Gatty, contributed position-finding by means of astro-sights on this, their first great flight together.

Anne and Charles flew east for another reason, to await the birth of their first baby. A son, Charles Augustus, was born on June 22, 1930 at the Morrows' family home in Englewood, under what amounted to almost siege conditions of publicity—the press considered that everything the Lindberghs did and every detail of their private lives were matters of public interest.

Chapter V ⇀ The Explorers

Early in 1931, Charles's thoughts turned toward an Arctic
survey flight, from New York to Tokyo and beyond, via
Alaska and eastern Siberia, as the basis of a future air route
for Pan American Airways. Because of the lack of landing
grounds in the Arctic, his Lockheed Sirius would have to have
pontoons fitted in place of its wheels, and a full range of appropriate emergency equipment would have to be devised and
procured. The fact that he now had to use a seaplane was
bound to introduce a number of new problems. For not only
does the en-route weather have to be suitable, but also the surface conditions (regarding roughness, smoothness, or obstruction by ice or tidal conditions) have to be favorable at the precise moments of departure or arrival. On the water there are
also the frequent dangers of being rammed by curious boat-
men, uncharted shoals ripping the pontoon bottoms during
landing or takeoff, mooring in strong currents, which may
drag the pilot out of his cockpit, and even an Eskimo paddling
his kayak under the aircraft when it has been fueled to capacity, then preparing to light his pipe. Launching and recovery

by an aircraft carrier can also be disastrous if wind and current are adverse. These are only a few of the extra worries the seaplane pilot may have on his mind.

While preparations for the long flight were being made, Charles gave Anne flying lessons in a Bird airplane at the Long Island Aviation Country Club. By all accounts, he was a strict instructor, even with his wife. At the end of May, Anne had completed the ten hours of solo flying needed to obtain her private pilot's license. She had also been undergoing instruction in radio and the use of Morse code, to enable her to keep contact with ground stations while flying across the Arctic wasteland.

The Lindberghs looked on their Arctic venture as a welcome break from all the troublesome publicity at home as well as a valuable contribution to air-route pioneering. The Lockheed Sirius, now equipped with Edo pontoons, had a 610-h.p. Wright Cyclone engine, which gave it a top speed of 185 m.p.h. and a still-air range of 2,100 miles. Normally, a plane having as high a maximum speed as 185 m.p.h. would cruise at about 140 m.p.h., but Charles deliberately chose to keep down to 118 m.p.h. for two reasons: one was that the lower power required would load the engine more lightly and therefore reduce the risk of breakdown, the other that it would cut the fuel consumption rate to only twenty gallons per hour, thereby improving the air-miles-per-gallon and effective range. There can be no doubt that the Sirius, designed by Lockheed to Lindbergh's specifications, was the most advanced and practical seaplane of its kind in the world at that time.

The start was delayed by both the usual technical snags that arise before a long flight and the delays in obtaining foreign flying permits, so that July was almost over before they got off. Having been down to Washington, on July 30, 1931, the Lindberghs dropped in at North Haven, Maine, where they had arranged for baby Charles to be left in the care of Anne's parents at the Morrows' summer house. Their next leg was to Ottawa, and there the Canadian authorities tried to persuade Charles to alter his route to Moose Factory to what they thought would be a safer route, dotted with habitation. (Curiously enough, the Canadians did exactly the same to me in 1934 when I wanted to fly straight across the Adirondack Mountains to Albany. I gave in to the authorities, but not Charles!) However, Charles threatened to fly east to Greenland if the Canadians would not let him use the overland route he had chosen, and the officials, realizing that such a route would be much more dangerous, reluctantly granted his request.

At Baker Lake, Charles and Anne first spotted Eskimos; thereafter, husband and wife took turns at the controls. The next hop was 1,270 miles west to Aklavik. This took 11 hours, 35 minutes and was made largely over a gray, treeless wasteland in the daylight of the Arctic night. Arctic fog and rain accompanied them to Fort Barrow, where they were unable to refuel because the annual supply ship was stuck in the ice some miles away.

They had encountered no darkness since Baker Lake, and Charles was surprised that night began to fall as he headed south for Nome. A combination of fog and lack of fuel forced him to land downwind, in the half-light, in a lagoon. There he discovered—by the way the anchor rope floated—that he was in no more than three feet of water. In fact, he was quite lucky to have landed safely. (I once pulled Charles's leg about this incident as being more appropriate to an inexperienced club flier than to an accomplished aviator, but he firmly maintained that the landing was all in keeping with his desire to try out his emergency equipment for an overnight stop, al-

A photograph presented by Charles to Anne and inscribed "To Anne
S. Morrow, Sincerely, Charles A Lindbergh, Dec: 24, 1927, Mexico
City" (Anne Morrow Lindbergh)

Harry Guggenheim, who (with his father, Daniel) gave such invaluable financial aid to Robert H. Goddard, the pioneer rocket scientist, *(middle)* with Charles Lindbergh in New Mexico in 1935 (Esther C. Goddard Collection, National Air and Space Museum, Smithsonian Institution)

▲
▲
A Goddard rocket in its infancy at Los Alamos, New Mexico. During this flight on August 26, 1937, the rocket broke in half (Esther C. Goddard Collection, National Air and Space Museum, Smithsonian Institution)

◀
(Top) Charles and Anne Lindbergh during test flights of their Lockheed Sirius airplane (Lindbergh Papers, Yale)

◀
(Bottom) Awkward things that happen to seaplanes (in this case the Lockheed Sirius), and it's lucky if only an assistant gets a ducking. (Keystone Press)

The accident in which Charles and Anne had to jump to safety: the British aircraft carrier *Hermes* was launching the Sirius in the Yangtse with improvised tackle (H. O. Dixon)

The Lindberghs back on shipboard, fortunately none the worse after their immersion in filthy water (H. O. Dixon)

though he did add, "I probably would not have taken off if I had known that we would not have made Nome before darkness.")

The next leg—1,000 miles—was exciting because it would take the Lindberghs across the Bering Strait to Karaginski in Siberia, and the Russian reception was unpredictable. The welcoming party of Russians and a small bear were all very agreeable, however, and they were hugely amused by Anne's surprise in finding that she had crossed the International Date Line, thereby suddenly changing from Friday in Nome to Saturday in Siberia. Here, and at Petropavlovsk, the next stop, the Lindberghs were more impressed by the forthright and enthusiastic people than by the background pictures of Lenin, laborers, capitalists, and tractors.

Weather in the Japanese archipelago proved to be extremely treacherous, and Charles depended more and more on Anne's work with the radio to obtain weather reports and to maintain two-way contact, sometimes under very difficult conditions, with the outside world. On the 1,000-mile hop to Nemuro, the two became trapped by a storm ahead and fog closing in from behind. There were sinister black peaks protruding out of evil mists, and the sun shining on the top of the fog bank was no help at all. Charles slowed down and opened the canopy, telling Anne to wind in the aerial, before he tried to fly down the side of a mountain, where a small opening in the fog temporarily allowed the sun's rays to be reflected on the water. The fog kept closing and opening so that, at one moment, Charles was flying visually, and at the next, he was on instruments—a very dangerous condition, especially when there are mountains about. The first attempt to break through was unsuccessful, and he had to climb up once more to surmount the fog before trying again to win another round in the battle between man and nature. Another dive and more black

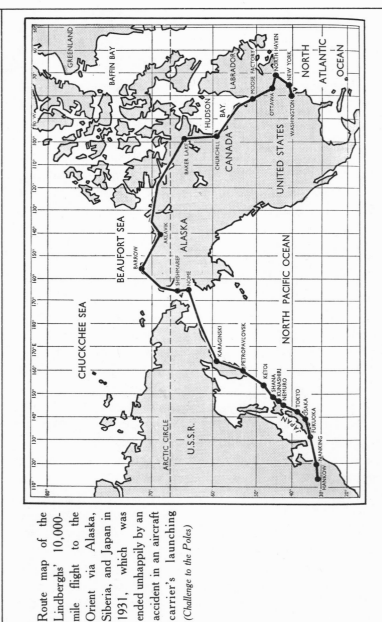

Route map of the Lindberghs' 10,000-mile flight to the Orient via Alaska, Siberia, and Japan in 1931, which was ended unhappily by an accident in an aircraft carrier's launching (*Challenge to the Poles*)

rocks appeared at such close quarters that yet a third climb had to be made to the top. Now Charles flew to another peak in the hope that conditions might be better near it. Diving down the side of what was evidently a volcano, with rocks and shrubs rushing by at close range, he suddenly spotted a tiny patch of sea over the edge of a cliff. He tore past the cliff, determined to reach the water. He came close to it but could see so little that he had to attempt a landing straight ahead. The water was very rough, and he made a series of bounces so hard that the spreader bar between the pontoons was bent. As he lost speed, he was relieved to find the plane was still maneuverable. He therefore tried to get to calmer water, as he heard the waves crashing on the coastal rocks nearby. In taxiing ahead, heavy seaweed became entwined around the pontoons. The moment they felt they were in the lee of the land, Anne dropped the anchor and, by rigging up an aerial on the wing, managed to transmit a message to Nemuro. The Japanese sent a ship to help the Lindberghs, and the sailors rigged up a temporary strut to hold the undercarriage in place. That was all right, but then the engine refused to start, for the battery was dead! On top of these troubles, Charles suddenly noticed that his plane was careening out of control because the anchor rope had been severed by a sharp rock, leaving the plane to drift rapidly toward the shore breakers. Fortunately, a launch from the ship dashed up, took the plane in tow, and pulled it out of danger.

A tornado was raging to the west, and the sea became even rougher, but Charles insisted on sleeping aboard the Sirius so that he and Anne could take action in the event of emergency. The next day, August 22, the ship towed the plane twenty miles to an area of more sheltered water, from which the Lindberghs took off for Nemuro, only to be dogged once more by blankets of swirling fog. Again Charles had to execute a quick and dangerous descent near mountains and carry out a forced landing on a stretch of water in such fog that he could not tell whether the body of water was a river or an inlet. After a wait of nine hours, he took off again and, this time, went right over fog-enveloped Nemuro. He had to turn back and make one more hazardous descent through a hole in the fog, so that he could lob down on the water. Here he managed to beach the plane among some reeds, and after another night on board, the Lindberghs succeeded next morning in reaching Nemuro with a half-hour hop. The weather improved, and they proceeded to Tokyo the next day. They stayed in Tokyo for three weeks before pressing on to Nanking, where they had heard that there was widespread hardship and famine caused by the disastrous flooding of the Yangtze. Charles therefore placed his plane at the disposal of the National Flood Relief Commission. On one sortie with a Chinese and an American doctor on board, they were so critically besieged by famished Chinese people after landing that Charles had to shoot over their heads with his revolver in order to make them withdraw.

From Nanking, the Lindberghs flew on to Hankow, where there were no lakes and the only place to land was on the swiftly flowing Yangtze. Here, fortunately, was stationed the British aircraft carrier *Hermes*, also on relief work, and she became a base for the Sirius. The slings and lifting tackle used for the carrier's own aircraft did not fit the Lindberghs' plane, so a set had to be improvised. The first recovery was successfully completed, as was the first launching. During the second launching, however, on October 2, 1931, when both Lindberghs were on board, the wind blew the plane at right angles to the current just as the pontoons touched the surface. The result was that a wing dug into the water. Seeing that things were developing fast, Charles ordered Anne to jump for it, and they both went into the water. Fortunately, they were pulled out very quickly by the crew of the safety launch, but the poor capsized Sirius was in a sorry state by the time it was back on the carrier's deck. The plane had to be sent home to Lockheed for a factory rebuild.

Thus concluded as long and difficult a flight as had ever been made by a float seaplane without preplanned intermediate assistance, and utilizing only existing harbors, radio stations, and handy bits of water along the 10,000-mile route between New York and Hankow. (Anne's exciting account of the journey was written in her best-selling book *North to the Orient*.) The fact that this air route was never subsequently developed was due more to Russian obstructionism toward international airlines than to the swirling fogs of the Arctic and Kurile islands!

Chapter VI ✈ The Tragedy and the Second Survey Flight

While still on the *Hermes*, the Lindberghs learned of the death of Anne's father, Dwight Morrow. Saddened, they sailed home and soon arrived at the Morrow house in Englewood.

In February, 1932, Charles and Anne moved to a new house in the open countryside at Hopewell, New Jersey. They had hardly settled in when the greatest tragedy of their lives struck. On March 1, baby Charles was stolen from his crib. The kidnaping was made more terrible because of all the publicity given to the name of Lindbergh, and the agony of two-and-a-half months' suspense before the child's body was found, even though a ransom had been paid. Anne kept an account of the opening stages of the heartbreaking affair in her diary, now a book titled *Hour of Gold, Hour of Lead*.

Naturally, after this stupefying tragedy, the Lindberghs moved and tried to isolate themselves more than ever. Fortunately, five months later, on August 16, 1932, Anne gave birth to the Lindberghs' second son, Jon, at Next Day Hill. Soon after this event, Charles began to plan another long flight for Pan Am, to take place the following year, with his Lockheed Sirius rebuilt as a seaplane again and fitted with a 700-h.p. version of the Wright Whirlwind. The route was to embrace the Arctic and the North and South Atlantics. Pan Am would provide a base ship to follow around in Greenland and Iceland. Juan Trippe's principal concern in this survey was to obtain as much information about potential seaplane harbors in all those countries that might lie in proximity to the North or South Atlantic and that could form a basis for the company's air routes of the future. In addition, the flight would extend to Leningrad and Moscow; this was primarily for political reasons, so that the U.S. government could benefit from the fount of good will that flowed on such an international basis toward the name of Lindbergh.

This time, the equipment had to be even more extensive in order to cope with conditions from inside the Arctic Circle down to below the Equator. Apart from the Pan Am–designed radio and direction-finding equipment, the aircraft was fitted with a Gatty ground-speed and drift indicator, to be operated by Anne over land, water, or ice. It required, however, that the aircraft's altitude be accurately known; thus, a periodic check had to be made by diving down to ground level and then climbing up again to establish the datum. This would be a difficult requirement over snow, the surface of which is often impossible to distinguish.

On July 9, 1933, the Lindberghs set out from College Point, Long Island, bound for Mrs. Morrow's house in Maine. They were seen off by such a gaggle of newspaper planes and other planes that one of them nearly rammed them over Long Island Sound, missing their aircraft by a matter of feet. After that, the weather became so foggy to the north that they had to cut inland in an unsuccessful attempt to find a clearing, which did not seem to exist, and in the end, just after passing Portland, Maine, Charles had to make a forced landing in a largish lake, which turned out to be South Pond. Here they used their outboard motor, attached to the spreader bar between the floats, to edge them gingerly toward shore, for the depth of the water was unknown. Then Anne repeated her trick of spreading the antenna over the wing so that she could send a message to Chatham, Massachusetts to say that they were down safely. She had been unable to transmit before because, owing to the weather, they had to fly so low that she had to keep the antenna reeled in. For a first day's gentle flying in home waters, it had been surprisingly eventful, what with the very near-miss with the other plane over Long Island Sound and weather so persistently foggy that Charles and Anne had been forced down in the fortunately placed pond. But they soon found themselves welcomed to a summer camp among the birches and enjoyed their night in the open air. Next day was fine for the half-hour hop to North Haven in Penobscot Bay, where Charles landed and tied up for one night only, so that he and Anne could finally bid farewell to baby Jon.

The flight to Halifax, Nova Scotia, took only two hours, and after a night there they had a hop of five hours to St. John's, over which Charles had last flown in such dramatic circumstances in 1927. They landed in Bay Bull's Big Pond, just south of the city. They hoped to continue next day to Cartwright, Labrador, where Balbo's "armada" of twenty-four Savoia Marchetti flying boats had just come in from Iceland on the previous day, but unfortunately the Lindberghs were held down by fog for a day and so missed the Italians. On July 14, Charles and Anne took off for Cartwright but dropped in en route at Botwood in order to refuel and see what kind of a harbor it was. After the great bluffs and cliffs of Newfoundland, Cartwright, with its low, unspectacular mountains, seemed like the end of the world. Everything—the cliffs, the shore, and even the water—was gray, and the inhabitants of the few scattered houses could muster only a single horse among them.

The Pan Am base ship *Jelling* awaited the Lindberghs at Cartwright, and they stayed a week in order to make a local survey, which included a flight over the mountains to see if there were any potential alternate sites, either for seaplane bases or for airfields.

When Charles and Anne wanted to start for Greenland, there was such a flat calm that their Sirius refused to take off, thereby compelling them to wait another day, and even then, Charles had to jettison fifty gallons in order to get off. Although the weather was fine at first, the crew encountered a solid wall of fog only forty miles away and was compelled to land at Hopedale, where the country was almost treeless and looked even more like the end of the world than did Cartwright. After a few hours, the weather cleared enough to allow another start. They aimed to go to Hebron, two hours up the coast, and as they flew, the scattered icebergs and growlers gave way to continuous pack ice, like a white shore. They had crossed the tree line, so that the scenery on land consisted of barren rocks, liberally supplied with clouds of mosquitoes. The Lindberghs found citronella oil only partially effective and were glad the weather was good the next day, July 21, so that they could be on their way to Godthaab. At 8,000 feet, they saw Greenland's icy mountains from about 300 miles off. On landing, they were greeted by a three-gun salute from the settlement's aged cannon and welcomed ashore by Danes and brightly dressed Eskimos, who in the evening put on dances to the accompaniment of accordians and fiddles, after the manner of the old Dundee whalers, from whom some of them were descended.

On July 23, Charles and Anne flew northward to Holsteinsborg, skirting the ice cap at close quarters on the way. The first settlement at which they landed turned out to be not Holsteinsborg (which is just inside the Arctic Circle), so an Eskimo directed them to the northwest, where they soon found the harbor, which they proceeded to use for aerial exploration over a period of eleven days. Their first out-and-home flight of four hours was along the edge of the ice cap to the northeast of Disko Island, and the second went to the eastern extremity of Baffin Land, where storms and thick fog drove them back.

On August 4, the Lindberghs finally left Holsteinsborg in an attempt to fly across the ice cap, a feat hitherto accomplished only by their compatriot Parker D. Cramer in a Packard diesel-engined Bellanca, and Wolfgang von Gronau in his twin-engine Dornier flying boat. The Sirius climbed toward Disko Island and turned in to the ice cap at Christianshaab, where there was every indication that the fine weather was stabilized.

After seventy miles, Anne later recorded her impression of the scenery thus: "The mountains behind us on the coast were sinking fast below that white dome. Still black on the horizon, soon they would be submerged from our sight. Ahead nothing but dazzling white, a white that had no depth or solidity, but looked like clouds or fog under a glaring sun."

An hour later, the Lindberghs were flying by dead reckoning under a high overcast without any visible landmarks. Lack of a horizon gave the impression that they had been lowered into a bowl without sides or even physical dimensions. With the canopy open for better vision, both cockpits became extremely cold, and even though she sat on her feet for warmth, the radio operator regretted that she hadn't put on a third pair of gloves in addition to all her other heavy clothing.

At the halfway point, they were at 11,500 feet but could not pick out the surface of the snow. Charles handed Anne a note that read, "Every five minutes we save a day's walk." The note was encouraging. Anne busied herself with the radio and was able to pick up the *Jelling* as well as other ships all the way across. She soon found herself talking to the base of Dr. Lauge Koch, 200 miles north of Scoresby Sound, and was invited to land there, so Charles, with the ice cap* safely behind, altered course accordingly.

---

* No one who has not flown across the mighty stretch of Greenland's inland ice can imagine the feeling of utter loneliness and detachment that it engenders. When I made my attempts in the Fox Moth seaplane *Robert Bruce* from Angmagssalik in 1934, I remember what a time I had. To begin with, on the way over from Iceland I had been lost, and after a lucky forced landing in a fjord, had been found by Eskimos after a night out. My first try from Angmagssalik was frustrated by heavy cloud, and on the following day, so was my second. For the third attempt, the weather was marvellous, with not a cloud in the sky, and as I climbed along the coast at full throttle, I was absolutely fascinated by the scenery. The sun was blazing down on black rocks, glaciers and heavily ice-strewn sea as I flew toward the mysterious ice cap, just near where it was first crossed forty-six years ago by Nansen with five companions on foot in forty-two days.

So entranced was I by the scenery that I had reached the edge of the coastal rocks at 9,000 feet before I suddenly realized it was time to change fuel tanks. Thereupon, I made the movements as though in a dream, which was rudely terminated a couple of minutes later when my engine gave a couple of coughs and stopped work. As I began to glide I saw below nothing but jagged rocks and crevassed glacier on land, and an endless carpet of floating ice in the sea, with no hope of a safe forced landing anywhere. So I banged out an S.O.S. at top speed and then began to look around for the cause of my engine failure. Ignition switches and oil pressure were O.K., but oh, the fuel cocks! They were all three at "off," and I realized that I had turned the little one off without switching the main one on. Immediately I put it on, holding the nose well down so as to keep the propeller turning, and then joy of joys my engine came back to life. As fast as I could I tapped out "O.K., O.K." and finally looked down to switch the transmitter off, to find that I had never turned it on!

The Lindberghs found Koch's base on a little beach at the foot of high cliffs and received a hospitable welcome from the great explorer and his naval aircrews, who had sent one of their Heinkels to guide the Sirius in. Considering the long route by which he had flown, Charles's time of seven and a half hours for this journey of about 900 miles was good.

The next day, Charles and Anne headed for Koch's other base, a hundred miles to the north on Clavering Island, and the day after that, August 6, they turned south for Angmagssalik. The harbor of Scoresby Sound was so chock-a-block with ice that they were glad they had enough fuel to overfly it.

Even in Angmagssalik, the amount of ice was such that it was difficult to find an open space for landing, and the Lindberghs were relieved to arrive without hitting any growlers.*

Not satisfied with one successful crossing of the ice cap, Charles decided two days later to make another flight over the top, back to Godthaab by the same route that I was to

---

*Flying over the inland ice believed to go up to over 9,000 feet was an unforgettable sensation. The blazing sun made the ice ahead merge into the atmosphere so that there was no horizon, just as Anne had described, and it was impossible to tell how near below the snow surface was. When von Gronau had made his crossing and thought he was at least 1,000 feet above the ice, his radio operator reported that the aerial was dragging in the snow.

Never had I experienced such a feeling of loneliness and of being utterly cut off from the rest of the world. In the ice desert, the only company I had was the shadow of *Robert Bruce* following me faithfully, for better or for worse, over the all-embracing whiteness below. I felt like a pinhead in space, as though holding my breath in the hopeful expectation that somehow by the grace of God I should be allowed to live to see the other side of Greenland. And so it was that after what seemed an eternity of waiting—actually only just over three hours—I saw the magnificent fjordland of West Greenland spread out before my delighted eyes. Although I have flown under many different conditions from Arctic to Antarctic, no other experience has ever approached the crossing of the ice cap for the feeling of thrill and triumph that it gave.

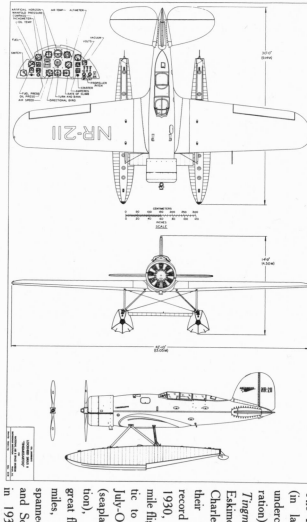

The Lockheed Sirius (in landplane fixed-undercarriage configuration), nicknamed *Tingmissartoq* by an Eskimo, used by Charles and Anne for their transcontinental record flight, Easter, 1930, their 10,000-mile flight via the Arctic to the Orient in July-October, 1931 (seaplane configuration), and their last great flight of 30,000 miles, when they spanned the North and South Atlantics, in 1933 (National Air and Space Museum, Smithsonian Institution)

use in the following year. From Godthaab, he popped down to Julianhaab, near Cape Farewell, on August 8 and back along the coast to Angmagssalik on August 12. On that occasion, the Sirius was christened *Tingmissartoq* by an Eskimo who painted the new name on the fuselage. *Tingmissartoq* means "the one who flies like a big bird," the cry uttered by the Eskimos whenever they saw the plane.

On August 15, the Lindberghs made their final bow to Greenland by flying first to have a look at Arctic explorer Gino Watkins' old base at Lake Fjord and then setting course across the Denmark Strait for Iceland.

At this time it happened that I was in Reykjavik with my De Havilland Gypsy Moth seaplane in which I was endeavoring to make a solo survey flight along the Arctic air route from east to west. When I heard that Lindbergh was in Angmagssalik, I sent him a cable offering to give any assistance possible in Iceland if he would let me know when he was coming, but there was no reply. On August 15, therefore, when the Sirius was expected, I was working in my hangar while an official reception committee awaited the Lindberghs at the harbor. As things turned out, the sea was so rough at Reykjavik that Charles decided the water was calmer near where I was and landed near my slipway. I ran out, commandeered a ferry, and towed *Tingmissartoq* to a mooring. Thus, I had the pleasure of my first meeting with the Lindberghs. Charles announced that they would sleep on board. Anne had been looking forward to hot baths, meals, and such amenities of civilization, and in the end, they took a walk to the village of Videy (on the island of that name, adjacent to their mooring) and were able to put up with a farmer in rural Icelandic style. Subsequently, they stayed at the same hotel I was in, and I saw them at meals. They also visited my hangar to have a look at *Rouge et Noir*. Charles presented me with the specially tinted goggles he had used for flying across the ice cap and later told Anne in private (as I learned from her many years afterward) that he was very worried about me because he thought I was sticking my neck out too far in trying to fly across Greenland in my 85-h.p. Gypsy Moth. Coming from him—who had stuck his neck out so much farther on his Paris flight in 1927—I think this was a very high compliment indeed!

Unfortunately, after being delayed by gales for several days, I eventually tried to take off for Greenland when it was still really too rough, and after two or three mighty bounces, I broke my undercarriage and capsized in Reykjavik harbor in the early hours of August 20. After attending to the beaching of my wrecked seaplane, I went to the hotel for a second breakfast with Charles and Anne and told my tale of woe to a very sympathetic audience. Charles sent his mechanics over from the *Jelling* to help me with salvage operations.

Charles insisted on preserving secrecy about where or when he intended to fly, so as to avoid giving the press any warning of where he could be found next. When the day came to leave Reykjavik (August 22, 1933), he first flew northwest across land to Akureyri, then doubled back to hit the south coast just east of the Westman Islands, and finally followed the brown lava beaches of the south coast eastward and round the corner to Isafjordur, where he lobbed in. After a night in this small fishing village, the Lindberghs took off for Thorshavn in the Faeroe Islands, which they found with all their cliff tops shrouded in cloud. Charles turned down a fjord—he later likened that experience to flying down a tunnel. Nothing could be seen above because of cloud, and to either side were the harsh, solid walls of rock rising out of the sea. Visibility was reduced because of driz-

Charles refuels his Sirius seaplane at Botwood, June, 1933
(Lindbergh Papers, Yale)

Anne tries out an Eskimo kayak at Holsteinsborg on the west coast of Greenland (Lindbergh Papers, Yale)

Greenland's only valley with a forest of willows and birches, near Julianhaab on the southwest corner of Greenland (Lindbergh Papers, Yale)

Tingmissartoq ("the one who flies like a big bird," named by an Eskimo in Angmagssalik) at anchor in Holsteinsborg on the west coast of Greenland, with the church in the background (Lindbergh Papers, Yale)

Escorted by Lauge Koch flying his Heinkel seaplane on the approach to Clavering Island (Lindbergh Papers, Yale)

Flying down the coast of Greenland: not much open water for forced landings here (Lindbergh Papers, Yale)

Angmagssalik, the east-coast settlement from which the Lindberghs flew to Iceland (John Grierson)

The Lindberghs come ashore near Reykjavik with the author *(hatless)* in the commandeered ferry. This was the first meeting of the two sea-plane pilots *(I Lofti)*

zle, and Charles wondered where on earth he could be. To make matters worse, the cloud came down almost to the surface of the water. Under a ceiling never more than 200 feet, he had an awkward time groping his way along until he suddenly found Thorshavn and was able to land outside the tiny harbor in some very choppy water. When the Lindberghs went ashore, they were told this was what the Faeroese called good weather!

Next day *Tingmissartoq* had a trouble-free passage to Lerwick, capital of the Shetland Islands, where weather forced the Lindberghs to stay a day before taking off for Copenhagen. Here, the Danes, having played hosts to the Lindberghs throughout their major tour of Greenland, very naturally wished to make a fuss about them on their arrival. But on Charles's insistence, they agreed that the Lindberghs would be given a "quiet time" in the Danish capital. However, when they landed, welcoming boats swarmed everywhere. After Charles had run his machine up a slipway, the Danish commander asked him if he and Anne would go in a motorboat to the harbor, meet the reception committee, and then drive to their hotel in an open car through the crowds. It would all be over in half an hour. But Charles refused pointblank. Parades were not for him, ever again. The Danes were absolutely dumbfounded and appealed to Anne for help, all in vain. Charles would have none of it. Everyone, especially Anne, was embarrassed, and the only concession was to go to the town hall for a private reception improvised by the mayor, instead of the originally planned open-air reception. This was an unfortunate episode, all the more so because it was not in Charles's nature to be inconsiderate of other people's feelings. In this case he caused resentment because of his unbending attitude.

On September 20, Charles and Anne went on to Helsinki

via Stockholm before the short hop to Leningrad. There the Russians made a point of according them VIP treatment, because they wanted such internationally famous persons to be favorably impressed by their contact with Communism. (This conflicted rather amusingly with my own solo appearance at Minsk just over a year before, when I had been cross-examined by the O.G.P.U. for four hours, and threatened with shooting as a spy, although my flight had been officially sanctioned and my fuel supplies actually laid down for me by the Russians at Minsk! I was honored by being assigned a Red Army man all to myself, who, with his bayonet fixed, accompanied me faithfully wherever I went —even when I went to wash my hands. Then in Moscow the whole inquisition was begun all over again, and it was only through the intervention of George Bernard Shaw that I eventually was allowed to fly myself to Astrakhan and Samarkand.) *Tingmissartoq* was welcomed to Leningrad by a formation of fighters, and in the following three days Charles and Anne had an intensive tour of the many palaces and visited the superb ballet. The sightseeing tour ended with a banquet. The wide boulevards reminded them of Paris, but Anne thought the people and many of the buildings looked drab.

On September 25, after being delayed by fog, they left Leningrad under a low ceiling and broke into open weather halfway along the railroad that carved its way through dense forests to Moscow, where they landed on the Moskva River. There followed another whirlwind tour of such places as the Kremlin, Lenin's tomb, an aircraft factory, and the Park of Culture and Rest, and another banquet was given them by the aviation people. The Lindberghs left Moscow on September 29 to fly to Tallinn, Estonia, where they landed in the harbor. Of her arrival, Anne wrote in *Locked Rooms and Open Doors,* "I feel as though a fever had dropped from me." After the pressures of Russia, she enjoyed spending a relaxed night. The next day, the weather was too bad to fly, but they managed to get through to Oslo on October 1. Here they were received by the King and entertained at an official dinner in the legation. Two days later, they crossed the snow-capped mountains to Bergen, where Charles wished to see the harbor, and then pressed on to Stavanger in the afternoon. On October 4, in dark and gloomy weather, they took off across the North Sea to England and managed to land on Southampton Water among all the busy shipping.

Anne's brother-in-law Aubrey Morgan met them in Southampton. After arranging for some work to be done on the airplane, the Lindberghs set off for a break in Wales with Elisabeth Morgan, Anne's sister, and were delighted that the local people understood their wish to be protected from the press. After a few days, they went to London, where Charles had some business, then returned to Wales for the weekend.

Anne was longing to go home to Jon, but Charles still had much work to do in visiting potential bases before they could cross the South Atlantic. They left Southampton on October 23 for Ireland and flew over Valencia Island, the point of Charles's historic landfall, before having a look at the Shannon estuary as a possible flying-boat base and going on to Galway. Then the itinerary was Inverness; Les Mureaux (a naval station on the Seine near Paris), where a man in naval uniform came up in a motorboat and greeted them on arrival in perfect English, "Good-bye, good-bye"; and Amsterdam. The Lindberghs then made a long flight to Rotterdam. Of this flight, Anne wrote in her diary: "I was in sheer physical terror the whole time." The weather forecast was grim, but

Charles had insisted on making the flight, declaring that in flying the mail he had often discovered that weather predictions were not accurate. But in the case of this flight, after hedge-hopping most of the way to Geneva in fog and swirling mist, Charles was forced to fly back to Holland. Anne would gladly have left that particular flight and gone home to America by herself; she knew, however, that if she did that, the papers would hint at divorce! Next day, they reached Geneva. On November 11, they flew from Geneva through fog, rain, snow, and storms, toward Vigo, in Spain. Once again, the weather looked bad, Charles was told that it was bad, and again he insisted on going. The clouds were not too low until toward Biscay, where there were storms with snow and heavy rain. Along the northern coast of Spain, the weather and visibility became so bad in the blinding, driving rain that Charles had to make a forced landing as best he could in the rough water at Santona, near Santander. During the night, the wind grew louder, and Charles found that his plane had dragged both anchors and was drifting along the pier, in grave danger of being smashed against it. He had to very quickly set two more anchors and make lashings to the shore as well.

The next day, the weather was still bad, but on November 13 Charles was once more determined to go. As Anne recounted in *Locked Rooms and Open Doors*, a man came out in a boat and shouted, "Storm at Vigo. You must not go." Charles shouted back, "We'll go see what it looks like." Accordingly, they went off into an overcast sky with local storms. Charles tried unsuccessfully to cross mountains to the south and was finally forced to follow a river in a valley, which led them on and on as the fog got worse, until he had no alternative but to land on the swiftly flowing water. He did so before Anne could wind in much more than half

Tvaeraa in the southernmost of the Faeroes, or "Sheep Islands," where the Lindberghs landed in drizzle under a 200-foot ceiling described locally as "good weather" (Lindbergh Papers, Yale)

The magnificent Faeroese cliffs, which tower nearly 3,000 feet out of the Atlantic and provide nesting for thousands of gannets and puffins (Lindbergh Papers, Yale)

Reception by Danish youths in the harbor of Copenhagen on arrival from Shetland (Lindbergh Papers, Yale)

Members of the Royal Danish Navy beach the Lindberghs' plane (United Press International)

Picturesque setting after an awkward forced landing in bad weather on the Minho River in Portugal (Lindbergh Papers, Yale)

Charles Lindbergh's photograph of the Portuguese photographers before breakfast on the Minho River (Lindbergh Papers, Yale)

the antenna. The result was that it was snapped off. They managed to anchor behind a sandbar and discovered that they had bypassed Vigo, ending up on the Minho River, the boundary between Spain and Portugal. Rather uncomfortably, they slept the night on board, and in the morning the weather was still bad, though, miraculously, a man arrived with gasoline. One more cold night they had to spend in *Tingmissartoq*, and on November 15, when the weather was more promising, they scraped the pontoon bottoms several times as they taxied upstream before reaching the takeoff position. Fortunately, they had no more trouble on the flight down the coast to Lisbon, where they landed on a choppy Tagus.

On November 21, they left for Horta in the Azores. En route, Charles and Anne shared the duties of taking sextant sights, which gave them a very accurate arrival. The harbor proved to be rather small, and for full-load takeoff, Charles moved the plane to Ponta Delgada, where the official motorboat nearly rammed them. Three days later, they went on to have a look at Madeira, and as Charles did not like the look of the heavy swell and lack of shelter, they proceeded to Las Palmas, in the Canaries. They then spent only one night before flying south to Villa Cisneros, the Spanish desert outpost immortalized in St. Exupéry's *Night Flight*.

On November 27, Charles and Anne headed for the Cape Verde Islands. On the way down the African coast, Anne had the thrill of contacting Long Island, at least 3,500 miles away, on her radio. This was a record distance between an airplane and a ground station. Porto Praia, Cape Verde Islands, turned out to have little shelter and a terrible swell, which Charles hit twice and bounced off before he finally landed. There was a very strong wind, which the locals said would go on blowing for six months without letup.

Nearly everybody seemed ill, some with tuberculosis, the majority with the "island fever." Almost as soon as the Lindberghs had arranged to be put up in the house of the Air France chief, they heard that it was "*toute contaminée*," with tuberculosis or some such disease, and there were bed bugs in the linen. After killing a few of the pesky creatures, Anne said that she could bear it no longer, so they went down and slept in the plane.

Charles realized that it would be impossible to take off from the eternal swell with more than half-load, so he decided to go back to the mainland of Africa before attempting the Atlantic flight. He cabled Dakar to ask permission to land, but they replied that there was a yellow fever epidemic. Charles then sought agreement from Bathurst, Gambia, as the best alternative, and was promptly accepted.

On November 30, Thanksgiving Day, the Lindberghs were towed out and tried to take off. The pontoons struck the water with the most terrifying of jerks and, as the bangs got more frequent, it seemed certain that something would surely break. Several times *Tingmissartoq* seemed to be flying, then fell back into the sea to the tune of more almighty bangs, until somehow at last she became properly airborne. What a relief to get away from that unhealthy stop!

At Bathurst, then a British colony, the aviators were looked after in style at Government House and were delighted to be in clean beds again. Charles learned that the problem here was exactly the opposite to the one at Porto Praia, because at Bathurst there was rarely any wind in the evening, which meant they would have to start in the morning. This was not very good because Charles and Anne really wanted to hit South America in daylight after the sixteen-hour crossing. The first morning's attempts to take off at full-load were absolutely hopeless. Then Charles jettisoned fuel, but by the time he was ready again, the wind had faded completely, and although he managed to get "on the step" this time, he never looked as if he were really going to fly. Activity was abandoned at this point until midnight, when Charles thought he would try a moonlight takeoff. Once again, the first attempt failed, and so did the second, and the third, until, in despair, the couple went back to bed.

Success in getting a seaplane to take off with a full overload of fuel always depends on favorable conditions, including broken water due to a fair breeze and not too much swell. They had taken off with the same load easily in Greenland, but here, almost on the Equator, in addition to bad surface conditions, the high temperature and humidity were seriously reducing the power of the Cyclone engine. Things had reached such a low ebb, Charles even thought he might have to put his plane on a ship to get home. That would have been the very last straw!

There was only one more night with enough moonlight left for another try, and, for that, Charles intended to lighten the aircraft to the very limit, leaving just enough gasoline to do the hop to Natal in Brazil safely. He decided, therefore, to remove one tank he was not using and every item of equipment he could possible eliminate. The anchor, tools, a tin bucket, and the chocolate they had been given in Greenland were all put ashore. Even Charles's razor was left behind!

And so, on December 5, after a run of over two minutes, during which the engine almost cut out but then recovered, the Lindberghs at last spanked their way into the air by the light of the tropical moon. They had had little sleep during the last two nights of takeoff attempts and should have been tired, but in the excitement of getting away that was forgotten. Four hours out, however, as she busied herself with the radio, Anne realized how hard it was to keep her eyes open.

But she had to contend with the tropical static that crackled in her headphones, making messages almost unreadable. They were running under cloud, which blocked the moon intermittently, until Charles was soon flying blind, the effect being accentuated by the darkness. Charles tried climbing until he reached a starlit sky, but not for long, and again the Sirius was shrouded in a higher bank of towering cumulus. At daybreak Charles reported eight-tenths of cloud cover, scattered squalls with visibility of three miles, and Anne relayed this to Porto Praia, back in the Cape Verde Islands, as they continued to fly through black thunderclouds.

A long message from Rio came in about the landing arrangements at Natal before they were halfway there. It seemed that as soon as it had got around that the Lindbergh plane was in the air, everyone wanted to pass them a message, including Chatham, Massachusetts, which tried to persuade the Lindberghs to give the first radio interview from an airplane! The answer, of course, was no because Charles and Anne were in fact far too busy for such a diversion even if they had wanted it.

Anne was taking time off from the radio to fly the plane as Charles wrestled with the sextant in front. She also took some sights through the Gatty drift meter and was surprised to see her husband pulling the sextant to pieces, though relieved when he had all the bits reassembled. Fortunately, the weather had improved and visibility was unlimited. Now contact was established with Luft Hansa's base ship *West-falen*, which was equipped with a slipway and catapult for picking up and refueling their flying boats at sea. The ship sent the Lindberghs a bearing while they were still 150 miles away, and this enabled them to fly right overhead to make a definite position check and set course to Fernando de Noronha, the huge volcano that sticks out of the South Atlantic

The last great Lindbergh flight of 30,000 miles, including both Atlantics and many European countries, in 1933

250 miles off the coast of South America. They soon found that desolate landmark. They hit the Pan Am station at Natal spot on, and there the air crew stepped out into a miniature U.S.A. Anne and Charles had completed the 1,890-mile crossing from Bathurst in 15 hours, 55 minutes, at an average speed of 119 m.p.h.

The most critical leg of the Lindberghs' survey had now been flown, and there remained only another 5,000 miles or so back to New York, if there were no digressions. However, after leaving Natal for a stormy flight of seven hours to Para (still in Brazil), Charles confided to Anne that instead of making a simple coastal and Caribbean Island itinerary back to New York, he wished to fly up the Amazon for 1,000 miles to an isolated town called Manaos because Pan Am was operating a service there.

There was bad weather over the Amazon delta—low cloud and fog—and the flying was again like that in Europe from Amsterdam, Rotterdam, and Santona. Fortunately, the clouds eased inland, and after passing a few villages in the jungle, the large city of Manaos was there in the middle of nowhere. After looking around for a day, the Lindberghs headed north, through squalls and across mountains, to Port of Spain, Trinidad, where low clouds down to 100 feet and heavy rain were once more the order of the day.

From now on the route home coincided with the existing air-route pattern and was for the Lindberghs more in the nature of routine than pioneering. On December 14, they forged ahead to San Juan, Puerto Rico, then to San Pedro de Macoris in the Dominican Republic, and to Miami, which was reached on December 16—almost home at last! They decided to break the 1,200-mile leg to New York with an overnight stop at the Navy yard at Charleston, South Carolina, where they had often been before. Finally, they flew into Flushing Bay, near College Point, after a flight of six hours, on December 19, 1933.

What a fantastic flight this had been! The Lindberghs, working as a team, had concluded a 30,000-mile survey—easily the longest ever attempted with a pontoon seaplane —without accident of any kind, although they had nearly been killed in a midair collision at the start on July 9; had had several near-misses with motorboats at various points; experienced some rather alarming forced landings in Maine, Holland, Spain, and Portugal; and on one occasion, at Santona, their *Tingmissartoq* was nearly wrecked by a gale. Over scenery ranging from the ice cap of Greenland to the jungles of South America, the Lindberghs had flown without faltering, and they penetrated some appalling weather on many legs of their route. This was not the sort of enterprise to attract sensational headlines because it was a feat of work without a trace of exhibitionism. For Pan American Airways, the Lindberghs discovered in just over five months far more air-route information than they could have found by any other means in five years, and the element of personal experience gave the joint enterprise a value that was unique.

Chapter VII ✦ THE RETREAT

Early in 1934, serious charges of fraud were being leveled at Postmaster General Brown in connection with air-mail contracts. T.W.A., with whom Charles was associated, was said to have been awarded a contract worth $5 million more than the bid of a rival. Of course, Charles, as their technical adviser, was not involved with the company's finances, and this was only one of many suspect air-mail agreements. President Roosevelt was so disturbed that, without waiting for specific charges to be made and responded to by the airlines, he canceled all the air-mail contracts and brought in the U.S. Army, who had neither the training nor the equipment to fly mail.

Incensed by action so arbitrary for the airlines and dangerous for the Army, Charles waded in with a very strong telegram of protest to the President. It was given nationwide publicity, and Charles's prestige caused his action to have serious repercussions for the administration. Charles's concern about the use of Army-trained pilots for mail-carrying was well founded. Several of those pilots were killed in crashes, and many had to make dangerous forced landings. The President's order had to be rescinded and the air-mails handed back to civilians in May, 1934, though on less favorable terms than had previously existed. This incident marked the beginning of the mistrust and eventual antagonism, never assuaged, between the President and Charles.

Although always deeply concerned with aviation and its progress, Charles had also, for some time, become interested in medicine. A stimulus to his interest was the illness of Anne's sister Elisabeth. She had been acutely ill as a child with rheumatic fever, which had left her with a heart condition for which there was at that time no cure. Charles began to investigate the function of the heart, nature's blood pump, and wondered whether it would be possible to devise some means of either assisting, or replacing entirely, the heart mechanism. Through the anesthetist present at the birth of his and Anne's first child, he had met the French surgeon Dr. Alexis Carrel, famous as a Nobel Prize winner for his work in physiology and medicine.

Carrel was working at the Rockefeller Institute, and when Charles sought him out and told him about Elisabeth, he said no operation would be possible without an artificial heart, and all attempts to provide one had so far been in vain. To Charles this was immediately a challenge and, as with his Atlantic flight, he would not take no for an answer. Under Carrel's guidance, he started to design and have made a perfusion pump that, unlike all previous attempts, would have immunity from infection. After several failures over a period of four years, Charles developed a successful pump in the summer of 1935. It perfused saline solution through the organ and kept an animal's tissue alive over a period of months.

Even though Charles was deeply absorbed by this work,

the publicity that he and Anne had tried for so long to escape was making their lives increasingly difficult. The ramifications of the trial of Bruno Hauptmann in 1935 renewed press curiosity about their private lives and even brought threats of kidnaping Jon. This was the last straw, so the Lindberghs decided to move to England and made a secret departure by freighter on December 21.

In London, they were guests of the elder statesman Lloyd George while waiting to find a suitable house. They finally rented a dignified and secluded house called Long Barn at Sevenoaks in Kent, which belonged to Harold Nicolson. After the first news of their arrival, the Lindberghs discovered to their delight that they were left in peace by the press. They were welcomed with quiet dignity by their neighbors and at Buckingham Palace. At one ball, because he was not a dancer, Charles enjoyed sitting out a dance with the Queen.

A less innocent invitation, although relayed to the Lindberghs by Major Truman Smith, the United States intelligence attaché in Berlin, came from Reichmarshal Göring. The Lindberghs went to Germany, where they were entertained royally and shown aircraft factories, research centers, and air bases in order to give them a terrific impression of the military might of the Third Reich. Charles's reports of everything he saw and heard in Germany were relayed back to U.S. Intelligence.

In the meanwhile, Charles had ordered a special two-seater touring monoplane called a Mohawk to be built with an American Menasco engine by F. G. ("Freddy") Miles, a well-known airplane manufacturer, at Reading. Of the plane's construction, Miles wrote, "Lindbergh was the perfect person to work for. I had a good deal of time with him and he knew what he wanted and just how possible it was to meet his wishes. He knew as well as I did the sort of compromises one has to accept when designing and making an aeroplane."

Charles flew the Mohawk to Ireland in December, 1936, in order to inspect the site of Shannon Airport, proposed as a trans-Atlantic base, for Pan Am, and then in 1937 he took Anne (who was expecting another baby) to India and back in the plane. This flight was described in part by Anne in *The Steep Ascent*, in which she gave a gripping account of the suspense and danger as they flew across the Alps to find Italy covered in cloud and fog. Soon after their return, Anne presented Charles with their third son, Land.

In June, 1938, after a visit to Dr. Carrel at his island home near Tréguier on the north coast of Brittany, Charles decided to move to a house in the adjacent island of Illiec. He thought that remote Illiec was the most beautiful place in the world and wished to move there so that he and Carrel could continue their experiments together. Living conditions, however, were so primitive—no electricity, telephone, drainage, or water except collected rain—that the Lindbergh family had to withdraw to Paris in winter.

Although he devoted so much of his time to scientific work, Charles continued to travel in Europe at the request of the American government because he was given ready access to the military aviation facilities of Britain, France, Czechoslovakia, and even Russia. Germany so impressed him—and Göring certainly had spared no pains in his showmanship—that Charles had come to believe that Germany could swamp all the other countries put together. At a Berlin dinner, which was being given by the United States ambassador so that Charles could meet with Göring and seek an improvement in United States–German relations, Charles was astonished when Göring presented him with the Cross of the Order of the German Eagle and Star, a civilian decoration for his contribution to the development of civil aviation. This award took Charles completely by surprise, and he could not refuse it in such circumstances. But he never wore the decoration.

Returning to London from one of his visits to Germany in 1938, Charles was invited to a meeting at the Air Ministry with the Director of Plans, Group Captain John Slessor, who in his book, *The Central Blue*, wrote, "In general, his attitude struck us as being entirely sympathetic to the British —so much so that one occasionally forgot that one was not speaking to an Englishman. He has an enormous admiration for the Germans, though he says of course there is much in their policy and methods which he cannot forgive." Recollecting that meeting today, Sir John Slessor writes, "He was a delightfully simple and honest man, I thought, but was not politically well versed in the tortuous methods of the Nazis. I would guess that he was properly sucked in by people like Göring."

Chapter VIII ✈ WORLD WAR II

Under the threat of war, Adolf Hitler summoned the prime ministers of Britain and France, Neville Chamberlain and Edouard Daladier, to a meeting in Munich with himself and Benito Mussolini in order to sign the notorious agreement of September 29, 1938, in which it was determined that certain districts of Czechoslovakia should be yielded to Germany, with guarantees of the new frontiers by all signatories. This moral capitulation was due to the disarmament policies of successive governments in Britain and France, leaving both militarily weak, and their fear of Nazi Germany, who had overawed them by ostentatious saber-rattling. The guarantees were utterly worthless because Hitler grabbed the rest of unhappy Czechoslovakia the following March. This was to prove, as everybody feared, that the Munich fiasco was only a postponement of the outbreak of a world war, which Charles as well as many others in Europe and elsewhere had been convinced was inevitable.

Following the final rape of Czechoslovakia, Charles returned alone to New York on April 14, 1939, in order to confirm to General H. H. Arnold, the commander in chief of the U.S. Army Air Force, his reports about the strength and preparedness of the German Air Force. Now, whereas Charles, as a Colonel in the Reserve Air Corps, was bent on furthering the rearmament of his country, he also felt that it was his patriotic duty to try to help keep his country out of the war, just as his father, when a congressman, had done in 1914.

Upon the outbreak of war in 1939, Charles saw Britain and France as allies who had failed to stop Germany when they could have done so and who then, having miserably failed to arm themselves, had declared war on Germany in honor of their treaty obligations to Poland, whose take-over they were utterly powerless to prevent. Finding themselves in a mess, Britain and France went on to appeal to Uncle Sam to pull them out of it.

Charles joined an isolationist group called America First and, owing to the mystique of the Lindbergh name, achieved such a following as to seriously embarrass the President, who had never forgiven Charles for the public outcry he had raised over the air-mail scandal. Charles's isolationism also evoked great bitterness from his own countrymen, and although his policy was most directly hurtful to the British, it was not so much from them as from his fellow Americans that he received the most acrid vilifications. He spoke out against Lend-Lease and made a speech in New York on April 23, 1941, in which he affirmed that America's duty was to stay outside the conflict and negotiate a peace to save the civilization of the world. He said in the speech, "It is now obvious that England is losing the war." He was nearly right because, on mathematical principles, the British *were* beaten but absolutely refused to recognize the fact.* Two

---

* Two factors unknown to Lindbergh were the British development of radar, which made their fighter defenses so effective; and their ability to break the German codes and thereby obtain vital information about the enemy's plans.

days after Charles's speech, at a press conference at the White House, the President almost accused Charles of treason. Deeply hurt, Charles resigned his commission.

When the Japanese attack on Pearl Harbor, on December 7, 1941, precipitated America's entry into the war, Charles still believed that his country should have stayed out and that the Japanese had been provoked because the United States had been so committed to helping the British and French with arms. Charles's inexperience and artlessness in politics led to widespread misunderstandings of his motives. Far from being pro-Nazi or anti-Semitic, his whole philosophy was based on a pro-American patriotism pursued to the point of fanaticism. But when the Senate voted to enter the war, he considered it his patriotic duty to serve his country, right or wrong, without reservation. He therefore offered his services to the U.S. Army Air Corps and was turned down flat. Thereupon he joined Henry Ford, the automobile manufacturer, doing his bit for the war effort by turning out airplanes, as a consultant and test pilot at a Liberator factory that was being built at Willow Run. At the outset, everything went wrong because the automobile men simply could not cope with the fastidiousness of aircraft production. In fact, the first sixteen Liberators to be made had to be scrapped, but by persevering in the retraining of operators and by adding a nucleus of skilled craftsmen, Charles succeeded in getting production into its stride.

He also held a consultancy with United Aircraft, makers of the Vought F4U Corsair fighter-bomber, which was used extensively by the U.S. Navy in the Pacific. He convinced the company officials that it was not sufficient for him to test-fly the airplane under artificial conditions, but he must try it out in combat. He was therefore issued a naval uniform bearing no badges of rank and was designated a "civilian

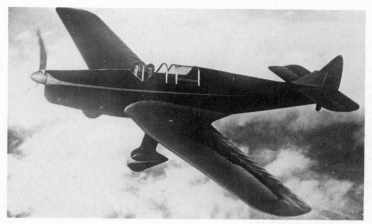

Lindbergh flies his Miles Mohawk, fitted with a 200-h.p. Menasco engine, which was built to his specifications at Reading, England (Lindbergh Papers, Yale)

Lindbergh discusses the engine installation of his machine with Miles technicians at Woodley Aerodrome, Reading, England (T. Miles)

Lindbergh, saying that England was "obviously losing the war," in his
New York speech on April 23, 1941 (Wide World Photos)

◀

(Top) Lindbergh, with the famous French ace Michel Détroyat, is
shown at a German aircraft factory

◀

(Bottom) The Lindberghs are received by Herman Göring at his Berlin home. Charles's reports of everything he saw and heard in Germany
were relayed to U.S. Intelligence (Zeitgeschichtliches Bildarchiv)

Lindbergh addresses an America First rally at Fort Wayne, Indiana, in October, 1941 (Wide World Photos)

▶

(Top) P-38 Lockheed Lightings flying over New Guinea (U.S. Air Force)

▶

(Bottom) Lindbergh and Major Thomas B. McGuire on Biak Island in 1944 (McGuire Air Force Base)

The B-70 North American supersonic bomber, nicknamed "The Savior," a bold experiment destined never to go into production (U.S. Air Force)

technician." In this guise and armed with a waterproof flash-light and pocket New Testament, he flew into Hawaii on April 26, 1944, and immediately went off for gunnery prac-tice, at which he proved a very good shot, having lost none of the skill from his boyhood days on the farm. For several weeks, he visited the squadrons and tested various airplanes on which problems had arisen. He then started operational flights from Rabaul on May 21. When a general pointed out that if he fell into Japanese hands he would be executed as a civilian, he replied that he felt that made no difference be-cause, according to reports, he'd be shot no matter what his status was.

On his first operational sortie, no Japanese aircraft were encountered, but there was heavy antiaircraft fire as Charles's formation dive-bombed and shot up their targets. This was the first of fifty sorties in which Charles took part, and although at the age of forty-two he thrilled at the dan-gers of diving low, sometimes in a F4U Corsair, sometimes in a P-38 Lightning, he could not help worrying whether some target might contain innocent women and children in-stead of the intended Japanese military. He was also con-cerned by his countrymen's treatment of Japanese prisoners on a basis of fair retribution and by their collecting morbid trophies, such as Japanese skulls.

In one "dog fight," on July 28, Charles shot down a Zero that missed ramming him head-on by less than ten feet. On August 1, he was saved in the nick of time from being shot down himself, thanks to the intervention of a wing-man. In his book, *The Wartime Journals of Charles A. Lindbergh*, only forty-one sorties are recorded, but this is the result of extensive cutting, and his logbook entries prove that Charles did the full fifty.

Apart from the combat flying in which he was personally

involved, Charles had also taught the squadrons how better to handle the engines of their Lightnings by reducing the r.p.m.'s and air speed so as to improve fuel consumption. On his arrival, the pilots dared only to operate at a range of 570 miles, but by using Charles's technique, they were able to extend the safe range to 700 miles.

At Roi Island, Charles not only fixed three bombs on a Corsair—the first time more than two 1,000-pound bombs had been carried—and dropped them on Japanese naval guns, but also devised a special rack to take a 2,000-pounder in the central position, thereby enabling him to drop a 4,000-pound load. He did this with such effect that by a direct hit he completely demolished a primary naval gun position. I remember his telling me about this in New York and saying it was a mere fluke, but the state of devastation was astonishing.

After his last operational flight, on September 13, 1944, he flew first to San Diego to see his friends the Voughts and give a firsthand account of the Corsair in combat. He then went to meet Anne, who had added daughter Anne to the family in 1940 and another son, Scott, in 1942, at a house she had just rented in Westport, Connecticut.

In May, 1945, Charles was invited to join a naval technical mission to investigate in Germany the development of jet aircraft and missiles. The Allies were of course anxious to obtain the maximum benefit from German brains and material in the aircraft industry and to prevent as far as possible their falling into Russian hands. In this respect, the Americans and British were rather like two schoolboys in an orchard, each intent on pocketing the maximum number of apples for himself. Charles remarked that, when he arrived, the British seemed to be everywhere, all intent on sending every technical specimen back to England. For example, Charles recorded in his *Wartime Journals* that in the B.M.W. engine factory at Munich, the mission was met by a young British lieutenant. When the mission had selected several interesting items to take back to Paris in their C-47, there was a "slight argument with the British about taking *anything anywhere* except to England. Settled by rolling up an American Army truck and loading in the items desired."

Charles was deeply impressed by the widespread bomb damage and the obviously starving state of the inhabitants. He also toured Camp Dora, near Nordhausen, where he was as shocked as other visitors by the furnaces used by the Nazis to burn their prisoners. Dead bodies littered around gave the place an atmosphere of stark horror. Men looking like walking skeletons lurked in the shadows. Charles later wrote in his journal the question many must have thought to themselves that day: "When the value of life and the dignity of death are removed, what is left for man?"

Chapter IX ➤ THE CIVILIAN AND BRIGADIER GENERAL

On his return to truly civilian life, Charles Lindbergh found little rancor from his friends, although bitterness persisted among the politicians. His great colleague Alexis Carrel, having gone back to live in France, had been condemned as a collaborator on entirely specious grounds and died a broken-hearted man.

Pan American Airways and Charles's old friend Juan Trippe welcomed him back to the company in whose service he had already contributed so much, to act as consultant, using him for special projects and investigations for future developments. He would, as he had since 1929, take a leading part in the approval and development of every type of airplane—including the new family of jets—to be used by the airline. He worked for a remarkably low salary, not because Pan Am was a bad employer, but because Charles had named the figure himself and would not agree to the raises the company proposed.

In 1953, Charles's *The Spirit of St. Louis* was published. This very detailed and well-written account of his New

York–Paris flight was widely praised by reviewers and won the Pulitzer Prize. Although it may seem surprising to us that Charles chose to write a book on a subject he had already described in another book twenty-five years before, it must be understood that *We: Pilot and Plane* had been produced under great pressure, for Charles had had to rush out the manuscript in three weeks. The result was a short, incomplete story narrated in such a hurry that Charles did not even have time to check it properly. He naturally felt dissatisfied with the early book and wanted to make good the resulting gap in history, which he did so well by writing *The Spirit of St. Louis.*

Charles served on the von Neumann committee to advise the Secretary of Defense on deployment and development of long-range ballistic missiles. He also inspected U.S. Air Force facilities throughout the world as special consultant to the secretary of the Air Force. In recognition of the important military role in which he was now operating, President Eisenhower appointed Charles a Brigadier General in 1954.

In 1958, a replica of the *Spirit of St. Louis* had been made for a film about Lindbergh, based on his book, with James Stewart in the title role. The plane was built by Paul Mantz, the well-known constructor of aircraft for the movies, who took immense trouble to fashion it as close to the original plane as possible. But when he came to fly the replica, Mantz was horrified by the result. Besides being blind, as expected, and like a vibro-massage to fly (because the engine was bolted straight onto the fuselage without any rubber), the controls were hopeless. The ailerons were so heavy, they were immovable at more than 100 m.p.h.; the elevators were abominably over-sensitive; and the rudder had very little effect at all. "I don't know where we have gone wrong," said Mantz. "Charles Lindbergh could never have flown the Atlantic in a heap like that. The only thing one can say is that it looks right."

It happened that one day Charles himself looked in on Paul Mantz and asked if he could fly the replica. Of course, Mantz did not want Charles to see what it was like, but could not very well say no. Charles took it up for over an hour, and when he landed, he shook Mantz warmly by the hand and said, "Do you know, I'd forgotten just how nice that airplane was! Of course it's a bit different to our modern standards, but you've got it just right. Thank you very much indeed."

In 1961, when I was embarking on a history of polar aviation, I wanted information from Charles about the two outstanding Arctic seaplane flights he had made with Anne as radio operator and navigator in 1931 and 1933. I asked him his rank—I was not sure whether it was Colonel or General—and he said he preferred no title because, as he wrote: "I feel that military titles are for military life. It is difficult for civilians to keep track of them and they tend to stiffen relationships and conversations." Although he was often slow to reply to my letters because of his extensive traveling—he wrote sometimes from Connecticut, sometimes from his chalet in Switzerland, or from North Africa or the Philippines—he always found so much mail awaiting his return. He helped me a great deal and did me the honor of writing a foreword to my book.

In 1962, when I had flown up to the U.S. Air Force base at Thule to do research on the book, Charles invited me to stay with him and Anne at their house in Darien, Connecticut. The visit gave me an enjoyable opportunity to discuss many subjects, beginning the moment we met in the Pan Am Building. Charles was of course reserved in discussing his work for either Pan Am or the Defense Department but did mention that he had recently been to see the mockup of the very advanced supersonic bomber, the B-70, and asked if I knew that they called it "The Savior." I replied that I had never heard the nickname, and he then told me that everyone who went into the hangar for the first time and saw the mockup exclaimed, "Jesus Christ!"

When I asked if I might take a photograph of him and Anne in their garden, Charles answered, "Yes, if you do not let the press have it." I assured him this would not happen, but he added, "You never know what those fellows will get up to for a photograph."

A little later, an incident underlined more clearly than ever Charles's utter phobia toward publicity, for he had never forgotten the outrageous act of a press photographer who broke into the Trenton, New Jersey, mortuary in order to photograph his infant son's body. In 1963, the British Broadcasting Company (B.B.C.) was preparing a documentary film on ocean flying, and because they had heard that I knew Charles, they asked if I could persuade him to participate. As it was my understanding that the film would be serious history, it seemed just worth a try, although I was not very hopeful. Back came the answer: "I have never appeared on television and intend never to. . . . As far as press and radio publicity is concerned, I have had enough to last a lifetime and several reincarnations. Any up-to-date publicity is highly disadvantageous to the type of life I want to lead. If B.B.C. is going to do any historical film that touches on any of my activities, I do not know anyone I would rather have cover my part than yourself." Needless to say, I was highly flattered by the trust Charles placed in me, but rudely shattered when, on November 1, I saw the result of the film called "Trail Blazers."

Charles's marathon flight to Paris was well done, but unfortunately the producer thought it necessary to include details of the kidnaping up to the execution of Hauptmann, and film clippings of Göring entertaining Charles and impressing him with German military might. The film finished off with clippings of the speech in which Charles had said that Britain was obviously losing the war. There was nothing about his work at Ford with the Liberators or his combat flying in the Pacific.

Now, having asked Charles to participate in the film, I naturally wrote to explain what had happened. To my relief, he replied, "I would not worry at all about the TV showing of 'Trail Blazers' if I were you. My experience has been that the Press, and this pretty much includes radio and television, confuses and cheapens almost everything it touches. This is the main reason why I discontinued all Press contacts many years ago. If you worry about the responsibility of the Press, you will do an awful lot of worrying."

I was relieved not to be blamed for what had happened, but what a tragedy it was that so great a gulf existed between Charles and the media. They had indeed treated him and Anne badly, but Charles had never come to terms or even seriously attempted to come to terms with them and, because of that, had merely provoked their desire to intrude and invent. At the same time, he needed and was prepared to accept the advantages of publicity when he had a patriotic message to propagate, whether in the furtherance of aviation, the case of President Roosevelt's misguided action in the airmail scandal of 1934, the Lend-Lease controversy at the outbreak of war, or his America First activities when he wanted to keep the United States out of the European war. At the end of his career, he went to the media internationally on behalf of the preservation of animal species under the banner of the World Wildlife Fund.

With the benefit of hindsight, one may well ask today whether Charles's 1939 political views were as misguided as many thought. He believed that the real enemy of civilization was Russian Communism, but in Europe and America the majority of people were so horrified by the Nazis' imprisonment and murder of the Jews and Slavs that the thought of giving even the most passive form of assistance to Germany was utterly repulsive. On the other hand, the Western powers gladly allied themselves with the Russians because they were forced to fight the Nazis, and they closed their eyes entirely to the reports that under Joseph Stalin far more people were murdered than under Hitler.

Had the Western powers and America armed themselves to a really formidable extent, and stood aside while Hitler invaded Russia and exhausted himself in the process, the state of Europe might have been very much healthier in the end. Of course, all history is full of might-have-beens, but no one except the Russians can view the state of Europe today with any satisfaction at all. More than thirty years after the war was nominally over, we have a divided Germany and a divided Europe, with Russia armed to the teeth and increasing its range and stocks of arms almost daily and menacing the lives of people both from without and from within, while in Africa and elsewhere she pursues imperialistic aims. It may be arguable that Lindbergh's strategy would really have worked out, but it is certain that the way in which our leaders handled world affairs then has left us with a nasty aftermath.

I met Charles in New York in 1967 and showed him photographs of my recent trip to the geographical and geomagnetic South Poles with the U.S. Navy. The photographs included shots of penguins, which interested Charles. He told me how involved he had become in the campaign to

Charles and Anne in the garden of their old home near Darien, Connecticut, October, 1962 (John Grierson)

▶

Lindbergh with Paul Getty and H.R.H. Prince Bernhard of the Netherlands at a World Wildlife Fund meeting in London (World Wildlife Fund)

The author and Anne Lindbergh at the new house, "Tellina," built in 1964, where Anne gave the author so much assistance in the preparation of this book (John Grierson)

Reeve Lindbergh's wedding shows most of the large and good-looking Lindbergh family. Adults are *(left to right, front):* Reeve, Anne Feydy (kneeling), Anne Morrow Lindbergh, Susan (Land's wife); *(back)* Richard Brown (Reeve's husband), Charles, Land, Barbara (Jon's wife), and Jon (Julian Feydy)

A striking 1973 portrait of Charles by his son-in-law Richard Brown
(Richard Brown)

◀ A fledgling monkey-eating eagle—the largest species of eagle in the
world—is presented by Lindbergh to the Philippines Bureau of Parks
and Wildlife (John Nance)

Grandson Charles with his mother after the snowy flight mentioned in the Introduction (John Grierson)

Jerrie Mock, the first American woman to fly solo around the world, in her Cessna 180 *Spirit of Columbus*. She took only twenty-nine and a half days in March and April of 1964 for the 23,103-mile flight (National Air and Space Museum, Smithsonian Institution)

preserve wildlife since a safari he had made to Africa in 1964. He said that he intended to spend a greater portion of his time—although he was still very active with Pan Am —on wildlife preservation. One of the species he was keen on preserving was the blue whale, the largest mammal on earth. I had to apologize at that point because I had played a part in the diminution of the whale population when in charge of aircraft on the whaling factory-ship *Balaena*, which, in the 1946/47 Antarctic season, accounted for 2,135 whales. Our only excuse was that the operation was in aid of starving Europe. John Strachey, the British food minister, said at the time that, even if we finished off the poor old whale, the oil from ground nuts in the Kongwa region of Tanganyika would make good the deficiency. This was precisely the sort of natural imbalance that Charles was trying to prevent by international agreement.

Other wildlife in which Charles was particularly interested, and for which he worked in conjunction with the World Wildlife Fund, were the Javan bison in Indonesia, the Tamaraw buffalo, and the monkey-eating eagle—the largest eagle in the world—both of which are indigenous to the Philippines. There, Charles enlisted the sympathy of President Marcos, who responded in 1968 to the pleas of conservationists such as Charles by enacting legislation to protect these fast-disappearing species. Charles once summed up the creed of the conservationist in a speech to the legislature of Alaska: "I do not think there is anything more important than conservation, with the exception of human survival, and the two are so closely interlaced that it is hard to separate one from the other."

In the Philippines too, on the northeast coast of Luzon, Charles chose to visit the Agta tribe of primitive people, flying in entirely on his own in a small airplane and landing on a logging company's unused airstrip. Twice he stayed a week with the tribe, depending on sign language alone for communication. He lived with them, shared their food, and slept under the stars on a grass mat woven by one of the women. Writing in the November, 1972 *Reader's Digest*, Charles said, "After sunset, lying on my mat on the warm sand, I fell asleep under brilliant stars to the rhythm of breaking waves. I woke about midnight to find a boy curled up next to the embers of my fire. By dawn he had left, and a dog had taken his place." Charles was tremendously impressed with the simple life of these people, who were so self-sufficient and content. They hand-worked iron spearheads; knives, bows, and arrows they fashioned out of local trees. Their food consisted of fish, deer, pig, corn, roots, and berries.

But just as remarkable was that no conscious effort was required on Charles's part to merge with the life and ways of these people, from whom he felt the world could learn so much about the stifling complexity of modern civilization.

Chapter X ⤚ THE LAST FLIGHT

Mors janus vitae, "Death is the gateway to Life," was signified by Charles Lindbergh's earthly end as he moved toward the conclusion of a life that in so many ways was an example for others to follow and a challenge to be taken up by the young people of today who are eager to contribute to the world of aviation.

In 1972, after a routine checkup in New York, Charles was told that he was suffering from lymphoma, a disease that he was assured could be treated and arrested. Although treatment was successful for a while, he had to go to Columbia-Presbyterian Medical Center in New York again in the late spring of 1974. He was then informed by doctors that the disease had reappeared in a more deadly form, lymphosarcoma, cancer of the lymphatic system, and that he had not very long to live. Charles discharged himself, against the advice of his doctors, because he wished to spend his last days out of reach of television and the ballyhoo of publicity at his Hawaii home on the island of Maui. Although the doctors had told Charles that no airline would carry a man in his condition, Charles and Anne were given special accommodations at the rear of a United Airlines DC-8, curtained off from the other passengers.

Charles wasn't afraid to die, but it irked him that, whereas on the many occasions when he had been face-to-face with death he had always had something to do, he now could only lie and wait. To keep himself busy, he therefore proceeded to arrange every detail of his funeral service and burial with the same meticulous care that he took in preparing for one of his long flights.

He laid out the specifications for his handmade coffin and for the digging and stone construction of his grave, for which he selected an inscription from the 139th Psalm: "If I take the wings of the morning, and dwell in the uttermost parts of the seas; even there shall thy hand lead me, and thy right hand shall hold me."

Anne was beside him, of course, as she had been beside him on so many of his air voyages. She chose the prayers and Bible verses to be read at the funeral service, then asked Charles to approve them. In discussing suitable hymns, Anne proposed one that she thought would be appropriate. She sang it to Charles, who shook his head and said it was no good. Anne said, "But, Charles, the music is by Bach and you cannot do better than that." "The music is all right," said Charles, "but the words are corny." "Well, what shall we do?" asked Anne. "Let's just have Hawaiian hymns," said Charles, "and then nobody will know what they mean."

Charles died peacefully in early morning on August 26, 1974. At the funeral service, at the suggestion of the Hawaiian deacon, four unaccompanied voices led off with an old missionary hymn, "Saviour, like a shepherd lead us."

o   o   o

How can one sum up the complex character of a man who did so much more than make the flight that marked an epoch in aviation history? He was honest, naturally modest, sincere, a devoted family man of unshakable faith, and was endowed with an absolutely superhuman measure of stamina. Charles Lindbergh had both the solidity of the Swedish tradition and a young American's fervent patriotism that he was prepared to pursue at any cost.

Charles and Anne had a large, good-looking, talented family. Jon, the eldest, has made his career in the field of under-sea technology and fish-farming in California and Washington State. Land runs a large and successful ranch in Montana. Anne married Julien Feydy, who teaches at the Sorbonne in Paris. They are the parents of a boy and a girl. Scott, married to a Belgian artist, Alika, lives near Périgueux, France, where he has forty monkeys that he uses for behavioral studies, and he has successfully bred exotic simian specimens where all other attempts in Europe have failed. (Curiously enough, Charles Lindbergh had devoted so much effort to preserving the monkey-eating eagle, while Scott was preserving the monkey!) Reeve Lindbergh is married to photographer Richard Brown. She teaches school and is the mother of two small girls.

Charles's occupations ranged from farming and engineering to flying, almost every conceivable kind of which he engaged in; he was interested, too, in archaeology, while in his medical scientific work with Alexis Carrel he displayed inventive genius. After the war, when Carrel was dead, Charles's work was rediscovered, and at the request of the naval hospital in Bethesda, Maryland, he redesigned an artificial heart in plastic instead of glass. He was also keenly interested in rocketry and space travel, hence his association with Dr. Goddard and support for his work through his friends the Guggenheims. In his last years, Charles furthered the preservation of animals in danger of extinction, through the World Wildlife Fund and in association with President Marcos of the Philippines. He took sympathetic interest in primitive peoples. Throughout his life, Charles was a prolific writer; many, many files of his unpublished work exist in several places, including the library at Yale University.

But that 1927 marathon from New York to Paris will always stand out as one of the most remarkable flights of all time, and the courage, endurance, and ability of the solo pilot Charles Lindbergh will light his name like a torch through the corridors of history.

AFTERWORD • 175

Afterword

In November, 1975, Anne Morrow Lindbergh was invited by the Council President of the International Civil Aviation Organisation (I.C.A.O.), representing 132 member states, in Montreal to attend a ceremony at which she would receive, on behalf of Charles, the tenth Edward Warner Award, this being the organizations's highest honor. For the first time it was being given to an American. The Award consists of an inscribed gold medal and a citation. The citation for Charles Lindbergh read as follows:

TO CHARLES A. LINDBERGH

In recognition of his invaluable moral and material contributions to the development of international civil aviation.

His magnificent solo trans-Atlantic flight in 1927 was made possible by vision, dedication, courage, and technical knowledge of the highest order; it unveiled to the world the possibilities that international civil aviation offered and was the feat which inscribed the name of Charles A. Lindbergh among those of the outstanding pioneers of the modern world. It was, however, far from being his sole achievement.

During a life dedicated to aviation he pioneered international civil air routes, contributed to the establishment of operating procedures and safety standards, and exercised a profound influence on aircraft and engine development that helped civil aviation realize the potential that was only a promise when Lindbergh first took the air.

In accepting the medal and citation from the Council President, Walter Binaghi, Anne said:

It is a great honor to receive for my husband an award from this international organization that has been dedicated for over thirty years to the peaceful purpose of civil aviation.

The Award has a special meaning for me since it is named for your first President, a man who was a friend of my husband and whom he greatly admired, and whom I remember very well myself—Edward Warner. I am sure there is no body of men and women he would have felt more at home with or prouder to be honored by.

The early fliers loved flying for itself, for the art of flying, for the freedom and beauty of the sky, the adventure of life in the air. My husband once remarked that when he began his career, and knew how dangerous it was, he decided that if he could live through ten years of flying it would be more than equal to an ordinary lifetime.

But these early fliers also looked ahead in a practical way; they believed wholeheartedly in the cause of aviation. Aviation in those days was a cause. They believed in the future of air mail and the commerce of the air. They had practical objectives. Very simply, they wanted flying to be safer, faster, and extending ever farther; but as well as practical aims, they also had idealistic hopes.

The very first speeches that my husband made after his

flight to Paris in 1927 are full of these hopes. He believed that aviation would increase human freedom and it would be one of the great forces of the future to bring nations together. Once people traveled freely and swiftly, he argued, we would have more communication, greater understanding, and there would be less strife in the world.

As we all know, the practical and technical objectives of aviation surpassed the most fantastic dreams of air enthusiasts. The efforts of aircraft pilots, engineers, executives, and governments succeeded in webbing the world with airlines. As my husband wrote nearly twenty years ago, we live today in the dreams of yesterday.

But despite all that civil aviation has accomplished in the past fifty years, its fantastic growth, its enormous contribution to mankind in freedom to travel, in facilitating commerce and communications, in scientific and humanitarian work, it has not automatically brought about peace in the world. Wars have continued. But man's hope has a way of persisting or of being reborn.

I find it heartening that this organization, dedicated to the peaceful progress and orderly management of civil aviation, had its birth in the last year of World War II, and since that time it has grown both in the numbers of nations cooperating and in the scope of its influence.

Aviation of course is no longer a cause. That cause was won many times over, and there are new causes now. Perhaps even thirty years ago, when this organization was founded, one of the greatest problems of modern times was not as clear as it is today. Aviation illustrates this problem, but it is universal throughout civilization. *It is the fundamental question of how to use man's creations for the benefit of man himself.*

This is the basic aim of I.C.A.O., and your efforts

toward its accomplishment will have results far outside even the immense field of aviation. Then, the dream of my husband and that early generation of fliers may be close to realization.

So today I salute the work and the on-going aims of this organization as well as the pioneers who had the dream. And I extend my deep appreciation and that of my family to you for this tribute to one of those pioneers.

Thus did Anne Morrow Lindbergh in so few words sum up the way in which Charles's work fitted into the I.C.A.O. and the way in which the I.C.A.O. is framing its constantly developing and ongoing policy for the benefit of civilization.

What is the message to the young people of America?

Allowances must be made for the tremendous changes that have occurred, both in aviation and also in the way people live and think, over the last fifty years. In the days of Charles's youth, aviation was not taken very seriously by those outside, and inside the field the active ones had a lighthearted approach to their work. There were fewer restrictions and less formality then than there are now.

Today, flying is much more serious business. There is little more pioneering to be done and no longer is it possible to achieve fame by a single flight, however meritorious. The moments when the pressure relaxes are more infrequent. Everything has been speeded up; more and more costly aircraft crowd the airways every year. Under conditions such as these it would be disastrous for aviation to be anything less than well regulated and well controlled. It must be said, however, that the regulations and controls unfortunately reduce the fun!

Although the atmosphere and practices of aviation have changed so radically, the same qualities which made Charles Lindbergh stand out in his era are as valuable today. And of all his many excellent characteristics, one sustained him more than any other from his childhood days, throughout his flying career, in the utterly determined but unpopular line he took in politics, and so on, right to those last dignified moments in Maui. Other Lindbergh qualities—perseverance, integrity, and modesty—could not have survived without his *courage*, the key to his whole character. Of *courage*, Samuel Johnson wrote, "Unless a man has that virtue, he has no security for preserving any other."

The opportunities in aviation today are more varied than they were in 1924. Barnstorming, wing-walking, and the five-dollar joy-ride are gone forever. Instructional flights are more closely regulated, as are the criteria for airworthiness. Implementation of air-traffic control depends almost entirely on radio: it is almost impossible to fly without it. Biplanes and tailskids have almost vanished and would be difficult to operate on modern, hard-surface airfields, which often offer only two directions for landings and takeoffs.

On the other hand, the modern pupil pilot finds himself in the helicopter age, the jet age, the supersonic age, the space age. How aviation has enlarged its scope in the last fifty years! There is nothing dull about the picture of today's opportunities, although they are so vastly different, in character and scope, from yesterday's.

Helicopters open up an enormous field in the Arctic and Antarctic, in mountains and jungles, or on oil rigs, where no airplane could possibly land. Helicopters have entirely new uses in military aviation as gunships as well as transports. They are inherently more difficult to fly than airplanes, but by virtue of the fact that they can reach such otherwise inaccessible places, they offer more exciting opportunities than many other forms of flying. Perhaps the most invaluable and rewarding element of copter flying involves its use in the saving of human lives.

The advent of Frank Whittle's jet has put at man's disposal

a fast vehicle with range sufficient to fly nonstop the longest stages of the world's airways or, in the military field, to launch rockets or drop bombs at extremely long range. The use of turbines instead of piston engines is beneficial in reducing vibration and the fatigue it causes passengers.

Supersonic flight (flying at more than 760 m.p.h. near sea level or 660 m.p.h. above about 33,000 feet) is the natural follower of the subsonic jet. It has been commonplace in military aircraft for many years but has now become an international hot potato in the civil field because of our fear about possible environmental damage—the unknown effects of large airplanes flying at more than the speed of sound. On the ground, too, there are apprehensions about possible noise and shock-wave effects.

The space age has provided us with some of the most uncanny performances ever presented on a television screen, and it has been marvelous to sit in the warmth of one's home and see men hurtling through space or actually walking on the surface of the moon. These activities, especially the American examples, have been performed with such precision and general reliability that the enormous complexity and ingenuity of the science behind them has been masked. The total number of men who have ever traveled in space is still very small, but how many of them are remembered? Indeed, how many young people can even recall whether it was a Russian or an American who first traveled in space or stood on the surface of the moon, let alone remember their names! How different this field of pioneering has been compared to the personalized era in the days of Lindbergh's early flights. The whole process of traveling in space is so much a team effort that the importance of individual identification has lessened.

Young American flyers today are exceptionally fortunate to have the enormously wide scope of choices made available to them in national aviation, whether in military or civilian spheres. Women aviators are also no longer considered rarities as in the days of Amelia Earhart, but play a large part in contemporary professional and amateur aviation. (Don Lopez, showing me around the new Air and Space Museum of the Smithsonian Institution, reminded me of their meteoric rise when he paused to remark, "That's the airplane of the first American woman to fly solo around the world." That woman was Jerrie Mock, and the year 1966. Of course, the most marvelous veteran of all flyers is Mrs. Marion Rice Hart, who goes on flying the Atlantic solo, even at eighty-three, as she always has done whenever "I find it rather boring at the kitchen sink.")

It is imperative to remember, however, that modern powered flight, in all its varieties, owes its prime origin to the Wright brothers at Kitty Hawk, and its demonstration and development to an army of pioneers, among whom the name of Charles Lindbergh stands on its own. Now the way ahead lies with the younger generation. They are the ones who, in drawing their inspiration from history, are going to carve out for themselves a future in the skies of the world, from pole to pole, and even beyond, in the realms of outer space.

Acknowledgments

I wish to express my sincere thanks to the following for their support and assistance: Anne Morrow Lindbergh, who, more than anyone, spared so much of her time to unearth photographs and check the text for me, and particularly for the splendid introduction she has written; Sir Peter Masefield; Juan Trippe, Pan American Airways; A. W. L. Nayler, Royal Aeronautical Society; F. C. Durant and D. S. Lopez, Assistant Directors for Aeronautics of the National Air and Space Museum of the Smithsonian Institution; Lieutenant Colonel R. H. Fredette, U.S. Air Force Historian; Herbert J. Coleman, *Aviation Week*; Nils Tellander, World Wildlife Fund; Captain J. G. Kelly-Rogers, Irish Aviation Museum; Général de Brigade Aérienne F. Perrotte, French Embassy; Helen Wolff, Harcourt Brace Jovanovich; Shelia Innes, map and diagram artist; John Bagley, Aerodynamics Department, R.A.E., Farnborough; Bud Gurney and John Noble, friends of Charles Lindbergh.

Glossary of Selected Flying Terms

AILERON   A movable control surface located on the wing used to bank the aircraft.

AIR-SPEED INDICATOR   Indicator of the speed of an airplane with relation to the air, as distinguished from the airplane's speed relative to the earth.

ALTIMETER   An instrument for measuring altitude, which registers changes in atmospheric pressure.

BANK   To tilt and thereby turn the aircraft.

BAROGRAPH   A self-registering barometer.

BIPLANE   An airplane that has two main wings, one of which is usually above the other.

BOUNDARY LAYER CONTROL   The control of a thin layer of air next to and passing over an airfoil, with the purpose of improving aerodynamic effects.

DRIFT   The lateral motion of an airplane due to air currents.

FLAP   A hinged or extendable surface at the rear of the wing. Extended flaps increase lift and allow the aircraft to fly at a slower airspeed.

FUSELAGE   The central body portion of an airplane, which accommodates the crew and the passengers or cargo.

LANDFALL   The sighting or making of land after a flight.

LANDING-GEAR STRUTS   Wood or metal structures that support the fuselage, wings, etc., above the wheel, pontoon, or ski assembly.

MONOPLANE   An airplane with one main wing.

PITOT-HEAD   The open tube facing into the air stream that leads the air into the air-speed indicator.

PONTOONS   Cylindrical floats for landing an airplane on water.

SEAPLANE   An airplane that is designed to take off from and land on water, provided with floats.

SEXTANT   A direction-finding instrument that measures the angle above the natural horizon of a celestial body in relation to the observer's position.

SLIPSTREAM   The stream of air driven toward the tail of an aircraft by the propeller of the aircraft.

STALL   The condition of an aircraft when its wings lose lift due to insufficient speed or disruption of the air flow over the wings caused by such things as ice, hail, etc.

THUNDERHEADS   Rounded masses of cumulus clouds that often appear before a thunderstorm.

UNDERCARRIAGE   The landing gear of an airplane.

WOBBLE PUMP   Auxiliary hand pump used to supply fuel to the carburetor of an airplane engine when the power-driven pump fails.

Index